The Chaining of the Dragon

A Commentary on the Book of Revelation

Ralph Schreiber

STANSBURY
PUBLISHING
Chico, Ca.

The Chaining of the Dragon
A Commentary on the Book of Revelation
Copyright © 2004 by Ralph Schreiber
All Rights Reserved

First Edition
ISBN 0-9708922-5-X
Library of Congress Catalog Number 2004019746

Stansbury Publishing
an imprint of Heidelberg Graphics
2 Stansbury Court
Chico, California 95928
www.HeidelbergGraphics.com

cover photo by Mike Simpson

To my wife, Lillian, who because she loved to read brought home our first book on the Bahá'í Faith. This event initiated investigation and the will to memberships in this newfound religion.

Acknowledgments

That the Book of Revelation is in need of explanation has been well established over the centuries. Scholars have concluded, "no one knows what it means," my co-worker, John Gravelin, who studied for priesthood, had told me as I attended to the barbeque. But a desire to know exists. In a discussion of religion, the owner of the Hardware Store asked me, "what about the Book of Revelation?"

Only because of new information do I offer an interpretation. In this respect, I would thank those who, out of silence, have rejected my early attempts at forming its story. Also, I am much indebted to those who have given me positive encouragement. My friends, Bill and Esther DeTally, have on numerous occasions encouraged me to continue with this project. Pastor Jim Austin graciously commented on some preliminary construction details. The Reviewing Committee at the Bahá'í National Center, by their comments and suggestions, has been reason for significant improvements of this presented version. And the enthusiastic response to the near final draft by Dr. Niki Glanz has confirmed my sense of purpose in this work.

Contents

THE PROBLEM AND THE SOLUTION

PREPARATION

TRUMPETS OF HISTORY

LITTLE BOOK

ISLAM

PROCLAIMING THE WORD

Foreword

The Book of Revelation is one of the most remarkable and upsetting books in the collection of writings revered for nearly two millennia in the Christian West as the Holy Scripture. Brief as it is—no more than twenty pages in most editions of the Bible—Revelation has given rise over the centuries to the most passionate and diverse responses. It has inspired great art, from the "Hallelujah Chorus" of Handel to the poetry and sketches of William Blake. On the other hand, it has, especially in our modern world so influenced by scientific rationality, excited the disgust and rejection of many. The great 20th century philosopher Alfred North Whitehead proposed that Revelation, with its depiction of eruptions of powerful irrational forces from the beyond, be deleted from the Bible in favor of a more "civilized" text from classical Greece. Those church fathers who finally decided on the scriptural canon certainly succeeded in concluding it with a bang: few individuals who consider themselves spiritual or religious remain indifferent to the extremes of the Book of Revelation.

"Revelation" is itself, as a translation of the Greek title, a civilized watering down of the original meaning. The literal translation is "Apocalypse." In the Greek, this word refers to the unveiling, through John, a disciple of Jesus, of that which has been concealed, the final and sudden clarifying of the mystery of human existence. The book purports to uncover the true meaning of human history by depicting the events of the "end of the world" and the arrival of a "new heaven and a new earth." It does so in a series of visions, symbols, hymns, and brief, dense narratives which leave the reader quite breathless and overwhelmed if he or she attempts to go through them all at one or even several sittings. Through the centuries, thousands of commentaries purporting to help readers decipher what the book "really" means have been composed and published. Ralph Schreiber's work is a fascinating and moving contribution to this body of literature.

Many of the images of Revelation are of sublime beauty. But many others display terrifying, bloody, and cataclysmic violence. It is the latter which have caused many devout people of a more peaceable temperament to turn away from John's writing. Because *shalom*, or full peace with true justice and well-being for all, is frequently described in the Bible as the goal of God's creation and work, people concerned for the destiny of humankind have frequently been reluctant to face the message of its concluding book, which seems to convey that the final peace will not come without horrendous conflicts and mass destruction. A look at Christian history also reveals, however, that a number of radical social movements have availed themselves of the visions of Revelation to legitimate their programs for change—and sometimes their violent methods in bringing about such change. It is perhaps a measure of the darkness of our human condition that the understandings even of different groups within the Christian Church have clashed so forcefully over the Book of Revelation.

It is, then, no small thing when an adherent of an altogether different religious faith and tradition regards the Book of Revelation as important enough to merit detailed and lengthy interpretation. Ralph Schreiber comes to Revelation as a Bahá'í. The Bahá'í Faith is a new world religion by the measure of the centuries. Unlike many in the modern Christian Church, he neither turns away from Revelation because of its highly violent themes and images, nor is he content with the idea that this document describes what will happen all at once at some future time, indeed at the "end of the world." Instead, Schreiber contends that Revelation describes, in symbolic terms, which can be clearly interpreted, the actual course of human history, as we know it. In this, the author is expressing the distinctive Bahá'í point of view, which is that history is a series of *progressive* acts by God through which He brings humankind to ever-higher levels of unity, wholeness, and fulfillment. This book is a beautiful example of the Bahá'í vision of God's preparation of humanity for Himself, his Glory, and his Law. The preparation occurs precisely through the various great religious traditions as God causes them to come to birth, one after another, in the course of history. Perhaps no other religion on our planet has been so consistent and insistent in assigning a positive role in the divine plan to all the *other* faiths, as has the Bahá'í Faith in the short 150 years of its existence.

And yet the author understands very well that progressive revelation does not and cannot mean that the great spiritual testimonies of the past can be left behind and forgotten. On the contrary, each one contains important clues to the meaning of history, because each of them comes from God. Thus the Book of Revelation, with its panorama of warring angels, plagues, dragons, the deepest corruption and the highest transformation, helps us understand what came later in the very historical stream in which we are all immersed. For instance, the rise of Islam, a faith which until recently was virtually ignored by the Christian Church but can be so no longer! This book, as documented by Bahá'í writings, claims to find the emergence and significance of Islam delineated in a book of the Christian Bible as something positive and meaningful for Christians and all human beings.

Another example is the coming of the Bábí revelation and of Bahá'u'lláh. Schreiber to Bahá'u'lláh applies the images in Revelation, which Christians interpret in terms of Christ's heavenly transfigured existence and His expected return at the end of all history. Christ's return does not mean, on this understanding, the end of history and the beginning of eternity, but rather the end of an era followed by a new and higher stage of human historical existence illuminated by this latest of God's great prophets, Bahá'u'lláh. Schreiber interprets, correctly in my view, the cosmic reach of Revelation's images as referring to the increasing globalization in a spiritual sense which the peoples of our planet are experiencing in these days.

Schreiber's work has opened my eyes to a lack in the Christian understanding of history. We have not been diligent in finding biblical and theological meaning in what has happened since Jesus was among us on earth. We have not seen the hand of God or His heavenly host in the day-to-day, year-to-year, century-to-century events of our existence, but instead have consigned these to some profane realm apart from the divine leading and acting. Even though his expression of theology is at variance with current Christian formulations, Schreiber's work enables us to grasp again the profound significance of the Book of Revelation, to regain the sense that the book is of the most immediate relevance to our religious, cultural, economic, and political lives. Reading Schreiber stirred again in me the deep excitement and sense of hope I once felt about the direction of events on earth. He helps us see again that even the deepest darkness, the deepest woe is for the sake of growth toward a full union of all humanity with one another in God.

May this book be but one of many in which the great Faiths carry humanity further into our glorious future by seeking out and finding new treasures of truth and meaning in one another.

Rev. Dr. Jeffrey Utter

Introduction

This commentary is about the Book of Revelation, which is the last book of the Bible. The Revelation of Saint John the Divine that never has been explained with certainty is about the road to the promised Millennium. Although only Chapter 20, out of twenty-two chapters, refers to the Millennium, and then only indirectly without use of the identifying name, it is demonstrated that the Book of Revelation is about this expected event. Past views on the Millennium have not been decisive as to whether the phenomenon will occur on earth, in heaven, or in both places, and much discussion has been made over when it should occur. These unresolved issues have been clarified because of the Bahá'í writings, which offer essential information on this subject.

As an aid to understanding, some explanation of this Faith is offered: The Bábí Faith like Christianity which had been raised from out of the Jewish Faith, was born on May 22, 1844 AD from out of the Islamic Faith. This momentous event occurred 2 hours and 11 minutes after sunset in Shíráz, Persia when the Báb announced His mission to Mullá Husayn His first believer and champion of His purpose. The Báb, Prophet-Herald of the Bahá'í Faith, proclaimed that He was the "mouthpiece of God Himself promised by the Prophets of bygone ages,"[1] which message and its implications were not kindly received by the combined religious and secular powers of His native country. Six years later He suffered martyrdom at the hands of a regiment of 750 riflemen. Today He is honored by the Shrine of the Báb on the slopes of Mount Carmel located within the grounds of the Bahá'í World Center. During the course of His ministry He thoroughly forecast the coming of One greater than He to whom all Bábís should turn. Although He, as with John the Baptist, held the precursor function, His station and rank was in fact Prophet of God; His Revelation and actions uniquely close the "Prophetic Cycle" and open the "Cycle of Fulfillment".

Bahá'u'lláh, the Báb's successor, became aware of His station as Prophet of God, nine years following the declaration of the Báb, in 1853. His given

---

[1] Shoghi Effendi, *God Passes By*, Bahá'í Publishing Trust, Wilmette, Illinois, p. 6.

name was Mírzá Husayn 'Alí-i-Núrí. Born of nobility and material well being, He refused privileges of class that with complete detachment He might actively participate in the Bábí Faith. One of His early outstanding achievements as a follower of the Báb took place in the hamlet of Badasht. Eighty-one disciples of the Báb were guests of Bahá'u'lláh for a twenty-two day period, an event that has become known as the Conference of Badasht. The conference occurred in the year 1848 during the early days of the Báb's imprisonment in the prison of Chíhríq, a time when He had won over the hearts of His immediate audience whose attendance over filled the courtyard of the prison. "'So great was the confluence of the people,' is the testimony of a European eye-witness, writing in his memoirs of the Báb, 'that the courtyard, not being large enough to contain His hearers, the majority remained in the street and listened with rapt attention to the verses of the new Qur'an.'"[2]

"The primary purpose of the Conference of Badasht was 'to implement the revelation of the Bayan by a sudden, a complete and dramatic break with the past—with its order, its ecclesiasticism, its traditions, and ceremonials.'"[3] This endeavor was successfully accomplished and perhaps to emphasize the enormity of the occasion, Bahá'u'lláh presented each guest with a new name and, without revealing its source, chanted a Tablet each day for the assembled believers. It was at this conference that Bahá'u'lláh assumed the name Bahá, which He later changed to Bahá'u'lláh.

About two years following the Martyrdom of the Báb, four years after the Conference of Badasht, the Bábí's had been thrown into a reign of terror because of the unlawful action of one young Bábí and his equally young accomplice. Distraught over the loss of the martyred Prophet, they attempted to take the life of the Shah who they believed was responsible for the death of the Báb. A reign of terror with unbelievable inhumanity against the Bábí's followed. "An Austrian officer, Captain Von Goumoens, in the employ of the Shah at that time, was, it is reliably stated, so horrified at the cruelties he was compelled to witness that he tendered his resignation." He stated in a letter, "'When I read over again what I have written, I am overcome by the thought that those who are with you in our dearly beloved

---

[2] Ibid, p. 20
[3] Ibid, p. 31...

18

Austria may doubt the full truth of the picture, and accuse me of exaggeration. Would to God that I had not lived to see it!'"[4]

Though Bahá'u'lláh was cleared of any involvement in the attempted assassination, He was, then again, known for His positive accomplishments within the Bábí movement and eventual became caught in the swirl of persecution. "During those somber and agonizing days when the Báb was no more, when the luminaries that had shone in the firmament of His Faith had been successively extinguished, … Bahá'u'lláh, by reason of the acts He had performed, appeared in the eyes of a vigilant enemy as its most redoubtable adversary and as the sole hope of an as yet unextirpated heresy. His seizure and death had now become imperative."[5] "Delivered into the hands of His enemies, this much-feared, bitterly arraigned and illustrious Exponent of a perpetually hounded Faith was now made to taste of the cup which He Who had been its recognized Leader had drained to the dregs. From Niyavaran He was conducted "'on foot and in chains, with bared head and bare feet,' exposed to the fierce rays of the midsummer sun, to the Síyáh-Chál of Tihran."[6]

Following other immediate persecution, He was incarcerated in that dungeon, which was known as the Black Pit. He was chained three flights underground in darkness and forced to share a common chance with thieves and assassins. In this loathsome atmosphere He received the first foreshadowing of His role as God's promised Prophet or Manifestation for this Age. Following release from the dungeon He was banished from His native country of Persia to Baghdad where He remained for ten years. Shortly before leaving Baghdad, following orders for further banishment, He sojourned with a select number of followers on an island in the Tigris River designated by Him as the Garden of Ridván. In this setting, He informed His immediate companions of His true Station; this event is now celebrated by Bahá'ís each year as the Festival of Ridván. Bahá'u'lláh was later banished to Constantinople (Istanbul), Adrianople, and on to the ancient fortified City of Acca situated across the bay from present day Haifa, Israel. His total ministry lasted for some forty years.

---

[4] Ibid, p. 65-6
[5] Ibid, p. 66
[6] Ibid, p. 71

He appointed His eldest son, 'Abdu'l-Bahá, by will and testament, Center of the Covenant to whom all must turn. In this capacity, He was successor and authorized interpreter of the Bahá'í Faith and given to demonstrate the qualities of a perfect Exemplar for all occasions. 'Abdu'l-Bahá has elucidated on many Christian principles much of which originated from talks He presented in Haifa, Israel as in *Some Answered Questions,* and from numerous talks He presented at the time of His tour across the American continent in 1912. These talks are presented in the *Promulgation of Universal Peace.* Although He had accompanied His Father throughout the years of banishment, His ministry as sole leader of the Faith was from the time of His Father's death in 1892 until His own passing in 1921. He allowed by will and testament the mantle of continuation to fall on His grandson Shoghi Effendi.

Shoghi Effendi's position is known as Guardian of the Faith. He guided the progress of the Faith, during its period of expansion throughout the world, and its concurrent formulation of administrative procedures. His various books are mostly assigned to history of the Faith, guidance for Bahá'ís and their communities, and on advice as regards problems and procedures of Bahá'í Administration. He was also engaged in developing the Bahá'í World Center in regard to its immediate and future needs. The Bahá'í Gardens on Mount Carmel, Haifa, Israel that evolved under his guiding hand, are known throughout the world.

Following these early figures as noted above, and to some extent concurrent with them, guidance and protection of the Faith was vested with appointed individuals. Known as Hands of the Cause, they had an indispensable role in maintaining the unity of the worldwide Bahá'í Community, especially from the time of the passing of the Guardian in 1957 until the election of the Universal House of Justice in 1963. Several of them at that time were elected as a group to collaborate in making arrangements for the first election of this institutional body. It constitutes the Supreme Executive and Spiritual Body of the Bahá'í Faith residing at its World Center in Haifa, Israel.

The Book of Revelation provides a perspective on the process of religious history that has led to that period generally referenced through numerous speculations as being the Millennium. Briefly alluding to Christianity, the Book of Revelation goes on to announce the arrival of the Faith of Islam, which it uses to develop symbolic themes of religious experience and concerns leading to initiation of the Bahá'í Era. The central proposition of the Bahá'í Faith, from its own writings, is the claim that it will inspire a world civilization developed by a maturing humanity and founded on the recognition of the oneness of humanity. Bahá'u'lláh explained that a global civilization is the highest stage of spiritual development open to mankind in this plane of existence. Thus it is that the Book of Revelation sketches an historical sequence of events and conditions leading to the Millennium and, through clarification of this same book from within sources of Bahá'í Commentary, explains the nature of this long sought after spiritual and social condition; the story of the Book of Revelation is developed by reference to various aspects of "God's Cause."

The term "God's Cause" includes all the divinely revealed religions of the world, such as Judaism, Hinduism, Buddhism, Christianity, and Islam. Each of them is a complimentary part of God's unfolding plan for humanity, and each Prophet-Founder of these religions holds the same station. Thus each major religion represents the phenomenon of religious renewal allowing for the continued spiritual development of humanity. One should note that the message of the Prophet in any given Era, Cycle or Dispensation, is commensurate with the contemporary level of spiritual development of its audience. This process of renewal is known by Bahá'ís as Progressive Revelation. Human development in this present age is destined, under God's guidance, to culminate in the establishment of world unity.

Humanity is inspired by the appearance of the Prophet and by the Word of God that He brings. Few people acknowledge His presence initially, but in time others participate and make for a creative process of spiritual renewal. Progress continues until the mid-day sun of acknowledgement when civilization is at its brightest for that dispensation. Beyond this apex of spiritual brilliance and with passing centuries, the light of civilization dims: loss of its past constructive spirit, coupled with the falling away from its institutions and their decline, brings atrophy even to the point of apostasy. By then the "last days" of a religious cycle have arrived, and the social condition becomes one of scriptural "woe."

Woe, at the end of a religious cycle, occurs at a period of time known by such terms as "the last days," "the time of the end," and the "end of the world." The concept has been obscured probably because a leaning toward literalism prevents understanding of the true meaning of this terminology. The period is known as woe because the light of good will has turned to a spirit of darkness and disunity of purpose and many social hardships exist within the environment; emphasis is placed on tradition because the true spirit of God's word is lost. Woe is a time when mankind has turned away from God's teachings, and appropriately, the condition calls for the return of the Prophet so that civilization can once more be renewed.

During the dark time of woe the next Prophet appears. Most people to the point of persecuting the Prophet and sometimes to His martyrdom reject Him. Persecution occurs because of the influence of vested powers and also because the Prophet never appears in a manner consistent with the generally accepted form of theological belief. Nevertheless, the Prophet removes the "veils" and "concealment" of the covered or hidden word. His function is to clarify and expose reality that has been presented in metaphor, which seems the only way of explaining new or misinterpreted concepts. That is why He comes in or on the clouds of religious doubt. Interestingly, this need for uncovering reality was apparently known to the ancient Greeks. About the Greek word "aletheia" it has been said: "It is surprising that so important a concept as truth has a metaphorical name in the Greek language ... the function of 'aletheia,' the function of truth, is very close to that of metaphor, because metaphor has the role of underlining certain aspects of reality, of making them shine."[7]

The religious process accounts for the stories of major figures of the Bible. Adam, Abraham, Moses and Jesus were all proponents of God's Cause. The Buddha, Krishna, and Muhammad brought the spiritual message of God to other regions and cultures, and it must be acknowledged that numerous other religions exist.

Bahá'í writings contain various commentaries applicable to unlocking the formerly hidden meaning of the Book of Revelation. Foremost of these passages, and the master key for partial understanding, is the commentary provided by 'Abdu'l-Bahá in Chapters 10 through 13 of *Some Answered Questions*. These chapters include His commentary on portions of the Book of Revelation; verses 5:7, 11:1-19, 12:1-6, and 21:1-3 are used in this work as verbatim presentations. The reader, looking for immediate evidence of interpretive accuracy and the direction of present remarks, is advised to begin by reading, pp. 105-120, the commentary on the Eleventh Chapter of the Book of Revelation as expressed by 'Abdu'l-Bahá. Additional aids to form-

---

[7] Edited by Stanley Romaine Hopper and David L. Miller, *Interpretation:* The Poetry of Meaning, Harcourt, Brace and World, Inc., New York, p. 43.

ing an overview can be had by reading the Summary, and from review of the Appendix, which presents prophetic time-span relationships.

Many other Bahá'í verses are quoted, and these help to fill out the story of the Book of Revelation. The quotations serve as strong foundations to the bridge of religious history, but finally, for full flow or continuity of each span, it becomes necessary to insert other material; this additional material is necessarily unconfirmed and contingent upon this author's understanding.

Various chapters of the Book of Revelation are grouped together in this commentary under the titles of nine individual headers, which the author believes represent the major supporting themes of the Book of Revelation. The totality of these themes seem appropriate to the flow of the message of the Book of Revelation, divulge the path of religion from the time of Christianity to the time of the return of Jesus Christ, and explain the Vehicles used for proclaiming the reality of the new heaven and new earth as promised in the Book of Revelation. The headers and their assigned chapters are as follows: The *Principals and Promises,* Chapters 1-5; *The Problem and the Solution,* Chapter 6; *Preparation,* Chapter 7; *Trumpets of History,* Chapters 8-9; *Little Book,* Chapter 10; *Islam,* Chapters 11-13; *Proclaiming the Word,* Chapters 14-16; *Old Social Order,* Chapters 17-18; and *New Social Order,* Chapters 19-22.

The author feels, as can be observed from the above headings, the predominant arrangement of the Book of Revelation is patterned after the concept of Progressive Revelation. Much repetition on this theme occurs within the chapters because they place emphasis, approached from different viewpoints, on normal characteristics of religious cycles and some of their history; religious cycles are the essential elements of Progressive Revelation. Some important subject matter within the pattern of Progressive Revelation observed by the author includes: the Voice of God, His Prophets and Religions, promised rewards for followers of seven religions who overcome, seven Spirits of God as seven Prophets identified as the Lamb, the need for religious renewal, prophecy of religious renewal, some history of religion, new scriptures as an element of spiritual renewal, the Islamic experience on the need for religious renewal, the Bahá'í experience toward religious renewal, plight of the old order, spiritual renewal being the Law of God married to the Word of God, comparison of the Millennium to a religious cycle, the new heaven and new earth as the renewed Law of God, and the association of God and His Prophets. Commentary presented by unsubstantiated material, where supporting scriptures is unknown or unavailable, attempts support to the flow of these subjects.

This author has gained much understanding from reading of the book, *The Apocalypse Unsealed,* by Robert F. Riggs and the book, *New Keys to The Book of Revelation,* by Ruth J. Moffett. They are now out of print; both commentaries were written from the standpoint of a Bahá'í Reference Frame. Robert F. Riggs has made a revision of his earlier works available on the Internet. To find, search for Bahá'í Prophecy Fulfilled, and under Christian Topics find "Apocalypse: An Exegesis of the Book of Revelation" by Robert Riggs. His work contains a profound amount of detail.

This present work places emphasis on what might be called the theology of renewal as noted above. It omits discussion of diverse esoteric symbolism of the Riggs' book, which is not essential for an explanation of the Book of Revelation as regards the path to the Millennium and to the understanding of its nature. In regard to both of the above books, this work lacks inclusion of personalized explanations available only to those who had early opportunity to visit the Bahá'í World Center. The attempt here is to present what appears to the author the orderly construction and message of the Book of Revelation. Its essential and exciting story discloses the approach to and significance of the new heaven and new earth. Understanding of this story in relation to events of history becomes, in itself, partial evidence for the interpretation, and the author hopes such understanding encourages increased participation in the path to the future.

Note that Biblical references within this commentary not having a book reference refer to the Book of Revelation, and italic quotations generally refer to the immediately preceding referenced verse or verses. Biblical references are taken from the King James Version of the Bible. Material within brackets […] inserted in quotations represents author's comment.

Unsubstantiated claims made within the section on summary, which follows, are explained in the later detailed commentary. The intent of the summary section is to present an overview on the Book of Revelation.

The Chaining of the Dragon

Summary

In every age and cycle He hath, through the splendorous light shed by the Manifestations of His wondrous Essence, recreated all things, so that whatsoever reflecteth in the heavens and on the earth the signs of His glory may not be deprived of the outpourings of His mercy, nor despair of the showers of His favors. How all encompassing are the wonders of His boundless grace! Behold how they have pervaded the whole of creation.

Gleanings, p. 62.

Summary

Principals and Promises

Chapter 1

   The Book of Revelation, a prophecy from God to John and last book of the Bible, frames a message about the return of Jesus Christ and of intervening history with commentary on those institutions that give support to His second coming. John of Patmos observes One like unto the Son of Man who relays the message. He sees that the Son of Man, a servant of God, holds in His hand seven stars noted as angels of seven churches and speaks as the Father. John is instructed to send the Father's message to the churches. The message invites people of the seven churches to participate in the future according to the plan and prophecies contained in the Book of Revelation. These prophecies have never been fully understood, and the fulfillment and nature of Jesus' return has been cause for much puzzling. Problematic to interpretation of this message is the use of extensive symbolic and metaphoric language in need of explanation. Yet beyond this barrier of hidden meaning the Book of Revelation provides a theology, which demonstrates that religion, itself, is a repeating process of renewal, atrophy, and renewal. The seven churches are shown to represent seven world religions all of which look for future fulfillment; participants from these churches, who recognize the return of Jesus, shall understand the prospect of the future and are invited to participate in spiritual renewal and the advancement of civilization as appropriate to the needs of this age of fruition.

Chapter 2 and 3

   Followers of religion who overcome, discover the return of Jesus Christ, and support God's Cause shall be rewarded. They are aware of the renewed Law of God, are enabled to contribute to the advancement of the spiritual/social state of society, and have the privilege of helping to revitalize the world situation at the time of His second coming. The seven churches, recipients of the message of the Book of Revelation, are shown in the first chapter to signify seven religions. The Book of Revelation, is then, seemingly addressed to seven churches but actually is addressed to the followers of seven religions of the world. The names of the seven religions, the reality of the churches, are identified as Sabean, Jew, Hindu, Zoroastrian, Buddhist, Christian, and Muslim.

Chapter 4

John is invited to heaven where he sees in a vision the participants of this legend. The one on the throne speaks as the voice of God with a voice as of a trumpet (1:9-11). He is the Son of Man (1:12-16) who shall appear at a later date as a Prophet of God in fulfillment of the return of Jesus Christ. Other participants include immediate followers, or apostles, and some individuals of secular origin but friendly to the Cause of God. Most significant are seven burning lamps before the throne that signify seven Spirits of God or the seven Prophets of the subject religions—significant because the concept of seven Prophets is proportionate with a theology of successive revelation harmonious with and serving the Cause of God.

Chapter 5

The heavenly scene continues with introduction of a little book that is closed by seven seals but if opened can explain social problems of both the past and present and lead to details of the future. After expressing concern about who is worthy, for no man had been found, general agreement of participants confirms that "the Lion of the tribe of Juda" is able to open the book. John sees Him in the midst of the heavenly setting as a Lamb having seven horns and seven eyes; His eyes signify seven Spirits of God, the Prophets, sent forth into all the earth, and His seven horns imply one name for each of the seven religions. The Lamb adds another dimension to the seven Spirits of God: He represents seven Prophet-Founders of seven religions and portrays the Prophet in the sacrificial plight of suffering persecution for revealing the Law of God. The Lamb takes the book from the occupant of the throne, and He shall expose by removal of the seals social conditions in need of restorative change. In response, the beasts, elders, and millions of angels sing a song (speak of) religious renewal. Impressed by the significance of this vision, all creation heard John bless and honor the throne and the Lamb.

The Problem and the Solution

Chapter 6

The Lamb, by removal of the first four seals, allows John to see four horsemen portray in metaphoric form some thoughts on the social condition. Their meaning depicts the ineffectiveness of religion including the problems of war, injustice, and spiritual indifference all of which is in need of correction so that humanity can enjoy a climate of good will amongst men. Elimination of the fifth seal demonstrates to John a difficulty occurring at the time of the Prophet's revelation: a hostile environment of vested interests always leads to persecution and martyrdom of some of those who hear the Prophet and work for renewal of the Cause of God. Martyrs from previous religious renewals and persecutions must be patient. Their plight shall be avenged at a later time, and during the interval of the delay until full renewal, there shall be many more who suffer and give up their lives for God's purpose. The end result of removal of the sixth seal shows that the day of wrath must come; it represents a time when the Prophet returns and reorders social condition, amounting to an earthquake of adjustment, so that people and institutions can be conditioned to fit the needs of an ever-advancing civilization. People of position and power indebted to the old order attempt to hide from the affairs of spiritual renewal. The effect of removing the seventh seal will be announced in Chapter 8.

Preparation

Chapter 7

John sees a great multitude of people who embrace the goals of the Lamb and are prepared to help God's Cause make a transition from the old order to a new order that is founded on precepts contained in the renewed Law of God. Preparation for social renewal is previewed and, in prophetic form, explains what must be accomplished. The winds of change, stressing need for adequate preparation in order to effectively alter the environment of the four horsemen, shall be held in abeyance until the appropriate time.

Social change requires sealing of servants, an elevating process that raises understanding (of the children of Israel) to spiritual maturity and prepares them and mankind generally for serving the Cause of God. Many followers with this enhanced understanding are required. The multitude, as seen by John, are from out of *tribulation*, which occurs when God's Word is renewed; all have been exposed to religious verities referenced as living fountains of water. The multitude understands the need for spiritual renewal as foretold in Chapter 5. Work within the new heaven and new earth for the building of a global society begins with the support of this following. Willingly, the servants are prepared to help at the time of Jesus' return.

Trumpets of History

Chapter 8

Previous chapters introduce the principal reformers and champions of God's Cause—the Lamb, Prophet, religious leaders, friendly beasts, and followers; describe the nature of social problems in need of resolution; and open the philosophy of change—a succession of religious dispensations. Milestones of actual history, foreshadowed by prophecy, are introduced as seven trumpets sound the course of history. The first four trumpets announce the direction of Christian history including the period of the dark ages (8:12). Following this review an angel flying through the midst of heaven confirms the continuation of the religious process by making known there exists three more trumpet blasts to come; these anticipate and announce three periods of woe following the Christian Revelation. Each period of woe appears at "end times" and carries burdens in need of religious and social renewal as previously indicated. The associated revelations and religions shall ultimately lead to the goal of humanity's acquiring spiritual qualities applicable to a global society.

Chapter 9

The fifth trumpet sounds an introduction to Islam; one element within Islam described as the bottomless pit symbolizes an early political difficulty within that Faith. Original enemies of Muhammad, the Umayyad Clan, create the bottomless pit of error from which they govern the Islamic state. Some connections between Christian and Islamic dispensation are noted by the sound of the sixth trumpet. It marks loss of powers previously bound to the Euphrates. Interpretation of timing indicates that 391 years[8] (9:15) following the fall of Eastern Orthodox Christianity because of Islamic warriors, the Dispensation of Muhammad ends and the second woe arrives. This second period of woe comprises the "end days" of Islam that give birth to the Bábí revelation in preparation for the coming of Bahá'u'lláh. Woe, p. 21, as used in the Book of Revelation refers to extreme social difficulties in need of spiritual correction.

Little Book

Chapter 10

Presented characteristics of the Prophet indicate that He appears, to many, clothed in the vision of clouded understanding; others see that He carries the covenant (rainbow) upon his head, is spiritually radiant as the sun, and always brings the Word of God by means of a New Book which is sometimes called a New Testament. The Book of God, presented with each new revelation, brings spiritual renewal. Especially, in respect to the Book of Revelation, its message foreshadows the time when the seventh trumpet sounds the Day of God and His mystery shall be revealed. John is instructed to read the little book because of its primacy, and told he must prophesy before many nations. The interlude of this chapter initiates those affairs that historically fulfill the "return" of Jesus Christ and bring corrective action to social conditions revealed by the four horsemen. Difficulties of the horsemen are further designated as the "bottomless pit," "pit of error," or "pit of ignorance," the substance of administrative depravity. Spiritual renewal revealed through the declaration of the Báb is associated with the second period of woe concurrent with the "last days" of Islam. The Báb is the precursor to Bahá'u'lláh. And when the seventh trumpet sounds the revelation of Bahá'u'lláh, the mystery of God shall be explained.

---

[8] See Appendix

Islam

Chapter 11

To acquire spiritual understanding and the well being of humanity, individuals should reflect on the nature of the Law of God; it includes both spiritual and social laws. The former such as love, charity, and trustworthiness are fixed and never change, while the latter are modified with each revelation to fit the needs of the day. Application of God's Law in the every-day outer court of daily practice may suffer when authorities are less than spiritual. The cited example is in respect to Islam; the Law of God had been trampled on for 1260 lunar years[9] (11:2). But during the same period of 1260 lunar years (11:3), the teachings of Muhammad had been central to Islamic society. Some Islamic leaders compromise the application of the Laws of Muhammad when they appeal to the pit of error. In consequence, the spirit of the teachings seems as dead bodies for 1260 years (11:9). At the end of this 1260-year period (11:11), revelation from the Báb beginning in 1844 AD brings a renewed spiritual message. The Báb, as Prophet, and Quddús, His chief disciple, are martyred and spiritually ascend up to heaven. With these events the second woe, period of the Bábí Faith, had ended, but the third woe comes soon. Nineteen years later, 1863 AD, the seventh trumpet sounds, and the kingdom belongs to God as manifested through His Prophet, Bahá'u'lláh.

Chapter 12

This chapter expounds on similar meaning while adding new information. The teachings of Muhammad, with the sun and moon of national connection, are championed by twelve Imams of Shí'ah Islam and symbolized by a woman, but the great red dragon of Islamic politics persecutes her. Islamic teachings, contained in the Qur'an, are protected for 1260 (12:14) years. Understanding, grounding in spiritual reality, rescues the woman. However, the dragon makes war with the remnant of her seed— those who recognize the Báb and Bahá'u'lláh and keep the commandments of God. At the end of the Islamic dispensation the woman gives birth to the Bábí revelation whose Founder, the Báb, is referenced as the "man

---

[9] Ibid

child." The latter appellation is prophetic of the Báb's youthful age of 25 years and the incredible content of His message. The Islamic teachings, recorded in the Holy Qur'an, carries on for 1260 lunar years[10] (12:6). Nineteen years later, 1863 AD, following the Báb, Bahá'u'lláh and His followers fight the dragon of ignorance. This effort continues and is preparing the way for salvation. Bahá'u'lláh's followers, many of which suffer for the Cause of God, are connected with and work with the Spirit of the Lamb. Those who look for spiritual renewal can rejoice, but woe—social difficulties and the wrath of God—unto the disbelievers.

Chapter 13

A beast, Mu'áwíyah from the Umayyad Clan, rises up from a sea of Islamic politics and indirectly causes the death of 'Alí, Son-in-Law of Muhammad; he gains control of leadership and compromises the application of Muhammad's teachings; his influence lasts for the 1260-year[11] duration (13:5) of the Islamic dispensation. This turn of events is discouraging to those who had suffered for God's Cause in the past. They must be patient. Their contribution is recognized, and others shall suffer at the time of spiritual renewal; then justice shall be served. A second beast comes with his father's understanding. Yazíd is the son of Mu'áwíyah and had carried on the same objectives and methods of accomplishment. He thereby secures the image of the beast. Yazíd is cause in the year 661 AD for the death of Husayn Who is the youngest son of 'Alí, the Son-in-Law of Muhammad. This tragedy had added to the developing cleavage between Shí'ah and Sunní Islam.

Proclaiming the Word

Chapter 14

A multitude of new believers, fulfilling the prophecies of Chapter 7, stand with the Lamb on Mount Sion; they had taken the name of the Lamb's father. The father's name is Bahá'u'lláh, and His followers are Bahá'ís. They sing the new song of spiritual renewal and religious unity that is symbolized by the sound of many waters and see the reality of past reli-

---

[10] Ibid
[11] Ibid

gious experience. By following the teachings for this age they give praise unto God and Bahá'u'lláh Who is His Prophet and Lamb. As announced by an angel, humanity is once more placed under the Law of God; the hour of God's judgment has come. Then it follows, as stated by another angel, the old order characterized as Babylon is fallen. Saints of the past who had suffered for the Cause of God must now be patient. Blessed are past martyrs; their contributions are recognized and shall later on be justified. The process of renewal had begun for it is time to reap; One like the Son of Man sat upon a cloud and has an ingathering sickle. Another angel follows him and also has a sharp harvesting sickle. The second and third periods of woe are merely nineteen years apart, the Bábí Revelation (1844 AD) is the precursor to the Bahá'í Revelation (1863 AD). Bahá'ís reap the vine of the earth, and the "winepress [had been] trodden" for those living outside the Law of God in the world at large.

Chapter 15

The transition period from the old order to the new order during the early phase of renewal is burdened with seven last plagues because many people reject the summons for renewal. But new believers, secure in their understanding and belief, stand on firm footing and partake of the qualities of Moses. Predictions claim all nations shall acknowledge movement toward spiritual renewal, and the books of God, renewed for this age, shall remain open. Angels had been prepared and initiate the seven last plagues of spiritual renewal; almighty God, the ultimate source of revelation, is the King of the saints.

Chapter 16

Events identified with the release of seven vials of wrath provide an historic sketch of Bábí persecutions and of Bahá'u'lláh 's banishment from His native land of Persia. New teachings question the current understanding amongst men, their sea of beliefs, and the powers of clerical authority. But this action is justified; the Lord is righteous because powers of the past had shed the blood of saints and prophets. Proclamation was initiated in Persia whose flag features that stellar body the sun. The process of rebirth opens the way for the Kings of the east, the Agents of renewal. The wrath of God challenges the common errors shared by all mankind. False prophets are troubling, but Bahá'u'lláh, working quietly, makes Himself known. Each vial of wrath counters social imperfections upheld by a sea of idle fancies and also releases spiritual power that works toward the goals of renewal. Understanding, amidst the people and past purveyors of the Word of God, must be altered to allow for spiritual and social transformation. This is the plan of God, and the prescription for change is justified. It is during 40 years of imprisonment and banishment that Bahá'u'lláh's writings had been revealed.

Old Social Order

Chapter 17

This chapter presents, in the form of a riddle, a repetition of material from Chapters 12 and 13. The quality and influence of Umayyad governance is now referenced as 'BABYLON THE GREAT, THE MOTHER OF HARLOTS AND ABOMINATIONS OF THE EARTH;' her lineage is from the bottomless pit of error. She wears the colors of religion and carries on in religion's name. In reality Babylon is full of abominations and filthiness; she it is who received the vials of wrath. Her dragon-like politics made war with the Lamb, but she shall be conquered by renewal of God's Cause. Babylon's territories, which gave her power, encompass the seven regions of the Umayyad Dynasty. Her fourteen kings and tribal chief have ten individual names, symbolized as horns, allowing one horn for each name; they hate the whore and had influenced her personality that is characterized as Babylon. God had put it in their hearts to hate the whore so that prophecy, as in the Book of Revelation, shall be fulfilled.

Chapter 18

Following the explanation of the mystery of Babylon, John sees the earth lightened by the Glory of God, Bahá'u'lláh, Who brings revelation and religious renewal in order to cure prevailing social shortcomings as is evidenced by the environment of the third period of woe. He is placing emphasis on the fall of Babylon and on the nature of some of its distressing qualities. His followers are advised to leave Babylon. Lack of spirituality, the running theme of the bottomless pit carries on, and many shall weep as sudden and difficult disturbances occur. Near continuous warfare of this century exemplifies her affliction. Dramatic mutations occur everyday as acceleration of social destruction approaches climactic proportions; the end of violence is unknown as the 21st-Century begins. The true spirit of the Word is difficult to find, and human virtues have mostly disappeared. Believers should rejoice for that great city will be reinstated in all its glory when a new heaven and new earth, designated as the Law of God, is acknowledged and married to a new order. And within Babylon is found the blood of prophets, and of saints, and all that had been slain upon the earth.

New Social Order

Chapter 19

Remaining chapters of the Book of Revelation place emphasis on the building of the new order that is referenced as a new heaven and new earth and otherwise known as the Law of God that has been revitalized and renewed for the needs of this age. Bahá'u'lláh's revelation identified with the third period of woe has inspired its spiritual qualities; spiritual laws and modified social laws fit the needs of a global society. The Law of God shall serve as a charter for an organized and united world, but administrative arrangements and culminating features are in need of acceptance by general agreement of the peoples and their governments. On this subject Shoghi Effendi has commented:

> The world is, in truth, moving on towards its destiny. The interdependence of the peoples and nations of the earth, whatever the leaders of the divisive forces of the world may say or do, is already an accomplished fact. Its unity in the economic sphere is now understood and recognized. The welfare of the part means the welfare of the whole, and the distress of the part brings distress to the whole. The Revelation of Bahá'u'lláh has, in His own words, "lent a fresh impulse and set a new direction" to this vast process now operating in the world. The fires lit by this great ordeal are the consequences of men's failure to recognize it. They are, moreover, hastening its consummation. Adversity, prolonged, worldwide, afflictive, allied to chaos and universal destruction, must needs

convulse the nations, stir the conscience of the world, disillusion the masses, precipitate a radical change in the very conception of society, and coalesce ultimately the disjointed, the bleeding limbs of mankind into one body, single, organically united, and indivisible.[12]

Praise of God from many people is unanimous, and righteous are His actions. Twenty-four elders and four beasts (religious leaders and friends) worship God that sat on the throne. The voices of a great multitude are saying Lord God omnipotent reigneth. Arrayed in fine linen, the Wife, that great city, New Jerusalem, is ready for marriage to the Lamb. Those who are invited to the marriage supper are blessed. The Lamb rides the white horse of conquest, and many crowns are on His head. He has been Prophet throughout the ages and because of sacrifice His vesture is dipped in blood. His name is called the Word of God, and His armies carry on with spiritual power; He shall smite the nations with the sword of His mouth. He controls the wrath of God, and He is the King of King and Lord of Lords.

Fowls that fly in the midst of heaven should join the supper of the great God; they can eat the material belongings of the kings. The beast from the bottomless pit and kings gather to make war; the beast and false prophets are cast alive into a lake of fire and brimstone. Remnants are slain with the sword from out His mouth, and the fowls are filled with the excesses of materialism.

Chapter 20

This Chapter accounts for the long lost Millennium paralleling the review of prophecy in Chapter 7 that anticipates transition to a global society. The Millennium, in reality, is a normal part of the religious process and represents a duration or dispensation that is more or less a thousand years long. It, as presented in this chapter, is constructed around the dispensation of the Bahá'í Faith. The historic significance and great importance of the Millennium can be visualized in relation to its goal of forming a spiritual humanity and world civilization nourished on the basis of the Law of God,

---

[12] Shoghi Effendi, *Promised Day is Come*, Bahá'í Publishing Trust, Wilmette, Illinois, p. 127.

renewed, and on recognition of the oneness of all mankind which condition shall be realized in its consummate golden age.

Spiritual rebirth, the result of religious revelation, holds for centuries, but toward the end of the dispensation, "last days" suffer loss of spiritual well being. Assurance of the people then rests solely on religious tradition or on non-belief. This is the condition of "end times" at which time the Word of God again comes to the rescue of humanity and removes the people from the pit of error by means of another Prophet and His message of renewal. This pattern of renewal is expected to continue in the future.

Chapter 21

John sees a new heaven and a new earth, referenced as New Jerusalem, coming down from God out of heaven. 'Abdu'l-Bahá explains that what John sees is the Law of God which assuredly comes from Him. It is also known as the holy city and the bride and is for all mankind because there is no more sea—the normal habitat of man is on the land. Significantly, the verses are saying the place of future holiness is with man, and that God shall dwell with the people. That is, they shall be aware of God and He shall dwell in their consciousness. Spiritual death and pain shall exist no longer for former feelings are passed away. Bahá'u'lláh, the Speaker on the throne, confirms He had made all things new. He told John to write: My work is done, and I am the beginning and the end and shall give the water of life freely to whosoever is thirsting. In fact, he that finds me shall inherit all things; *"I will be his God, and he shall be my son."* But those without any spiritual qualities, burning with fire and brimstone of remoteness, shall experience the second death. John is shown the Lamb's wife who is literally the Law of God renewed for world civilization and descended from God's heaven by means of the revelation of Bahá'u'lláh, the Glory of God; the Law of God reflects the brilliance of precious stones clear as crystal, and its message for all mankind is protected but open to view because of holy souls at the twelve gates of the holy city, three facing each direction. Values are upheld by renewed spiritual development. By measuring it with a golden reed, an angel proceeds to evaluate the holy city, the Law of God; it configures as a cube and is mindful of the true spirit of Islam and complete according to the measure of a man who in his essence is God's angel. The

Law of God is analogous to the beauty of precious stones and gold with clarity of glass and from the outside world is sometimes pictured as being too idealistic. God and the Prophet are central to the city, and there is no need for other light, for Bahá'u'lláh, the Glory of God, does lighten it. Nations and their leaders, those that are saved, shall walk in its light and bring their honor into it. It shall always be open, and spiritual values shall not be defiled therein.

Chapter 22

Pure spiritual teachings, noted as water of life, are seen by John proceeding from out the throne of God and the Lamb. In the midst of the throne and referenced as the Tree of Life is the Prophet whose teachings includes those spiritual and social concepts required for the healing of the nations; there shall be no more curse for servants shall allow no spiritual void. The throne of God and the Lamb shall be served by His servants who understand His expression and carry His name, spiritual qualities, in their demeanor; there shall be no spiritual darkness or need for candles. God gives the light of His teachings, and His servants shall reign forever; the Law of God shall be the ground for power democratically held by the throne. His angel shows things from the Lord God of the holy Prophet, which must shortly be consummated. Behold He comes quickly. Those who believe and hold to the prophecies are blessed. When John understands he falls at the feet of the angel, but He, the Speaker, Bahá'u'lláh, informs John that He is a fellow servant of John's brethren, the Prophets, and that John should worship God. The content of this book, its spiritual message and plan for the future, must be kept open for the time to understand and take action is at hand. The Law of God is laid bare, and mankind must not shun its responsibilities. Bahá'u'lláh comes quickly and awards according to the nature of one's activities; no need to change the character of anyone. He represents the eternal voice of God, and those who abide by His message, as revealed for this age, have the right to the tree of life and can enter, or be saved, through His holy souls at the several gates of the city. But those in the midst who ignore the Law of God are the doers of evil. The source of spiritual understanding is within the religions as testified by Jesus. Bahá'u'lláh is the root and the offspring of David as explained in Chapter 5. He as

Prophet, by means of His teachings, invites all people to take the water of life, the Law of God, freely. Those who hear this message shall not add or subtract from the meaning of this book of prophecy. The Law of God must be accepted in its entirety and not parceled out according to whim or vain imaginings of personal theology.

Principals and Promises

Chapters 1-5

It hath been decreed by Us that the Word of God and all the potentialities thereof shall be manifested unto men in strict conformity with such conditions as have been foreordained by Him Who is the All-Knowing, the All-Wise. We have, moreover, ordained that its veil of conceal-ment be none other except its own Self. Such indeed is Our Power to achieve Our Purpose. Should the Word be allowed to release sud-denly all the energies latent within it, no man could sustain the weight of so mighty a Revela-tion. Nay, all that is in heaven and on earth would flee in consternation before it.

Gleanings, pp. 76-77

Revelation Chapter 1

This Prophecy

The Revelation of Jesus Christ, which God gave unto him, to show unto his servants things which must shortly come to pass; and he sent and signified it by his angel unto his servant John: Who bare record of the word of God, and of the testimony of Jesus Christ, and of all things that he saw. Blessed is he that readeth, and they that hear the words of this prophecy, and keep those things which are written therein: for the time is at hand.(1-3)

The Book of Revelation, that last and usually misunderstood book of the Bible, records a vision from God, seen and heard by John, who was *"in the Spirit."* The message was given to him so that he could *"bare record of the word of God...the testimony of Jesus Christ, and of all things that he saw."* God *"sent and signified"* the revelation by one who has "the power of the confirmations of God, his angel."[13] The Book of Revelation is about prophecy and includes an appeal for action from the spiritually developed, recognized as angels, and "confirmed by the breaths of the Holy Spirit."[14]

John is the hearer and observer, and *"bares"* record of 1) *"the Word of God"* 2) *"the testimony of Jesus Christ,"* and 3) *"of all things that He saw."* Jesus Christ, by His testimony, confirms the truth of the Book of Revelation.

Blessed is the reader who is attentive, understands, and promotes the purpose of this prophecy and its urgent message. The directive is for servants of God so that the prophesied future can be attained.

Message From God

John to the seven churches which are in Asia: Grace be unto you, and peace, from him which is, and which was, and which is to come; and from the seven Spirits which are before his throne; And from Jesus Christ, who is the faithful witness, and the first begotten of the dead, and the prince of the kings of the earth. Unto him that loved us, and washed us from our sins in his own blood, And hath made us kings and priests unto God and his Father; to him be glory and dominion for ever and ever. Amen.(4-6)

---

[13] `Abdu'l-Bahá, *Selections From The Writings of `Abdu'l-Bahá,* Bahá'í World Centre, Haifa, p.166
[14] Ibid, p. 199

Initially, John offers grace and peace to God's designated servants, seven Churches, from three sources: (1) *"from him which is, and which was, and which is to come;"* (2) from *"seven Spirits which are before his throne;"* and (3) from *"Jesus Christ, who is the faithful witness."* For interpretation of meaning, the function of each source must be understood and any differences of particular qualities be made known.

"[H]im which is, and which was, and which is to come" designates the Eternal Voice of God that is manifested through His appointed Messenger or Prophet. He is beyond all entities, being the "Alpha and Omega, the beginning and the ending." (1:8) His Voice brings the Law of God. There are *"seven Spirits"* before His throne.

These *"seven Spirits"* before the throne are characterized as being like unto a Lamb as can be seen from the following verse:

And I beheld, and, lo, in the midst of the throne and of the four beasts, and in the midst of the elders, stood a Lamb as it had been slain, having seven horns and seven eyes, which are the seven Spirits of God sent forth into all the earth. (5:6)

Who are the *"seven Spirits of God sent forth into all the earth"* that are appearing before the throne of *"Him which is, and which was, and which is to come,"* and why are they compared to a Lamb?

Jesus Christ is the faithful witness and the prince of the kings of the earth. Throughout the development of Western Culture, Jesus Christ, the Lamb of God for the Christian Revelation, was the spiritual ideal and Savior of Christian Kingdoms.

Glory and Dominion

Behold, he cometh with clouds; and every eye shall see him, and they also which pierced him: and all kindreds of the earth shall wail because of him. Even so, Amen. (7)

Jesus Christ is sitting on the throne of power and will return in fulfillment of His "Second Advent," but most people, as an immediate response, are blinded to His arrival because of theological veils; He, therefore, *"cometh with clouds"* that hide His mission from the people. However, in time, *"every eye shall see him,"* even the enemies of spiritual renewal. They, *"which pierced him…and kindreds of the earth shall wail"* because of their belated recognition.

The Eternal Voice of God

I am Alpha and Omega, the beginning and the ending, saith the Lord, which is, and which was, and which is to come, the Almighty. (8)

The Eternal Voice of God presents His credentials; He is the channel of past, present, and future revelations, which suggests One speaking as the voice of the "Father." From repeated epiphany, peoples of the earth will continue to grow in spiritual well being.

Jesus Christ refers to His heavenly Father throughout the scriptures, but this relationship is in need of further clarification. The nature of God, and of the Father, and of Jesus Christ has been a point of contention throughout the development of Christian Theology. This subject matter, on the nature of Those Who speak for God, has been clarified by Bahá'u'lláh.[15]

I Am Alpha and Omega

I John, who also am your brother, and companion in tribulation, and in the kingdom and patience of Jesus Christ, was in the isle that is called Patmos, for the word of God, and for the testimony of Jesus Christ. I was in the Spirit on the Lord's day, and heard behind me a great voice, as of a trumpet, Saying, I am Alpha and Omega, the first and the last: and, What thou seest, write in a book, and send it unto the seven churches which are in Asia; unto Ephesus, and unto Smyrna, and unto Pergamos, and unto Thyatira, and unto Sardis, and unto Philadelphia, and unto Laodicea. (9-11)

John's vision because of its symbolism can be compared to a dream where, for understanding, it becomes necessary to interpret the meaning of various scenes and symbols. That John was in the Spirit on the Lord's Day is significant. The day could be the equivalent of Sunday, but in broader outlook is construed to mean that John's vision was of things to come at a time called the "Day of the Lord" which is the time of the Prophet and the renewal of religion. Such times initiate new religious dispensations. One objective of the Book of Revelation is to create awareness about a new

---

[15] Bahá'u'lláh, *Gleanings from the Writings of Bahá'u'lláh,* Bahá'í Publishing Trust, Wilmette, Illinois, Section XXII.

heaven and new earth that is, as later shown, the Law of God renewed. Visions of John refer to metaphoric descriptions of prophecy and intervening history all of which foreshadow the initiation of a new age.

John is commanded by a voice with the sound of a trumpet, the Eternal Voice of God—*"I Am Alpha and Omega"*—to write in a book what he sees and to send the message to seven churches. These churches are servants of God and are invited to participate in bringing to fruition the purpose of the Book of Revelation. They are discussed more fully in Chapters 2 and 3

For 19-Centuries the Book of Revelation has not been interpreted with certainty. Does not its message transcend the importance of seven ancient churches of Asia? Suggestions have proposed that the churches represent seven periods of Christianity.[16] Perhaps beyond Christianity, itself, the seven churches, as servants of God, have greater meaning as befits this message about the return of Jesus Christ and of the related spiritual renewal that will occur at that time.

'Abdu'l-Bahá has explained that the church is a symbol of unity for a religion, and even greater than the church the ultimate symbol of unity is the Prophet Who brings the Law of God. Because of this symbolism about unity, He refers to the church as a "collective center." History shows that the Jerusalem Temple was the point of unity central to the concept of the Kingdom of God and that the Synagogue replaced the Temple as the Jews were displaced from Jerusalem. Similarly, the church became the center of unity for the Christian Community. In the words of 'Abdu'l-Bahá:

> In the terminology of the Holy Books the church has been called the house of the covenant for the reason that the church is a place where people of different thoughts and divergent tendencies—where all races and nation—may come together in a covenant of permanent fellowship. In the temple of the Lord, in the house of God, man must be submissive to God. He must enter into a covenant with his Lord in order that he shall obey the divine commands and become unified with his fellowman. He must not consider divergence of races nor difference of nationalities;

---

[16] Uriah Smith, *Daniel and the Revelation,* Southern Publishing Association, Nashville, Tennessee, p. 361.

he must not view variation in denomination and creed, nor should he take into account the differing degrees of thoughts; nay, rather, he should look upon all as mankind and realize that all must become united and agreed. He must recognize all as one family, one race, one native land; he must see all as the servants of one God, dwelling beneath the shelter of His mercy. The purport of this is that the church is a collective center. Temples are symbols of the reality and divinity of God—the collective center of mankind. Consider how within a temple every race and people is seen and represented—all in the presence of the Lord, covenanting together in a covenant of love and fellowship, all offering the same melody, prayer and supplication to God. Therefore, it is evident that the church is a collective center for mankind. For this reason there have been churches and temples in all the divine religions; but the real Collective Centers are the Manifestations of God, of Whom the church or temple is a symbol and expression. That is to say, the Manifestation of God is the real divine temple and Collective Center of which the outer church is but a symbol.[17]

The Manifestation, often times known as Prophet, Son, or Friend of God, is the ultimate point of unity and servant of God; the Manifestation's followers, united by the "church," comprise other servants of God.

Modern communications and available expansive vision allows one to see all major Religions of the world. This universal view is in contrast to the constrained view of early regional or limited religious dispensations. In this regard, 'Abdu'l-Bahá, makes it manifestly clear by His commentary on Chapter 11 and the first six verses of Chapter 12 of the Book of Revelation, that the Book of Revelation is concerned, not only with Christianity, but also with the religion of Islam, the Bábí, and the Bahá'í Faiths. For symmetry of reasoning in addition to evidence provided above, the seven churches of the Book of Revelation can be construed as meaning seven Prophets and their seven religions developed from as many revelations and spiritual re-

---

[17] 'Abdu'l-Bahá, *Promulgation of Universal Peace,* Bahá'í Publishing Trust, Wilmette, Illinois, pp. 157-158.

newals. The message of the Book of Revelation addressed to the servants, the churches, becomes an invitation for all the followers of these world religions to participate in the future that is destined to lead to the development of a global society. The subject of *world unity*, manifested as a global society enjoying *world peace*, is the central feature and ultimate goal of the promised new heaven and new earth, a term that signifies the Law of God.

He Had In His Right Hand Seven Stars

And I turned to see the voice that spake with me. And being turned, I saw seven golden candlesticks; And in the midst of the seven candlesticks one like unto the Son of man, clothed with a garment down to the foot, and girt about the paps with a golden girdle. His head and his hairs were white like wool, as white as snow; and his eyes were as a flame of fire; And his feet like unto fine brass, as if they burned in a furnace; and his voice as the sound of many waters. And he had in his right hand seven stars: and out of his mouth went a sharp twoedged sword: and his countenance was as the sun shineth in his strength. (12-16)

An all abiding inclusiveness of the message can be seen because the *"one like unto the Son of man,"* who speaks for God, stands in the midst of *"seven golden candlesticks"* that indicate seven churches (1:20) and symbolize seven Religions and their followers. The Son of Man is clothed with a long garment, wears a *"golden girdle,"* has hair *"white like wool,"* and stands on radiant feet.

> In this radiant century divine knowledge, merciful attributes and spiritual virtues will attain the highest degree of advancement.[18]

The description of God's anointed, except for the qualities of radiance that are appropriate for all God's immediate representatives, does not fit the appearance of Jesus Christ who was but thirty three years of age at the time of His death on the cross. Seeing *"[H]is head and hairs were white like wool, as white as snow"* seems not a befitting vision and expectancy for one of that age. He returns in a different physical body! Apparently, the "return of Jesus Christ" must be fulfilled by the Son of man according to the experience following Jesus' radiant transfiguration on an high mount. His disciples,

---

[18] Ibid, p. 126

Peter, James and brother John, questioned Him as they were returning from the mountain.

> And as they came down from the mountain, Jesus charged them, saying, Tell the vision to no man, until the Son of man be risen again from the dead. And his disciples asked him, saying, Why then say the scribes that Elias must first come? And Jesus answered and said unto them, Elias truly shall first come, and restore all things. But I say unto you, That Elias is come already, and they knew him not, but have done unto him whatsoever they listed. Likewise shall also the Son of man suffer of them. Then the disciples understood that he spake unto them of John the Baptist.
> (Mat 17:9-13)

Jesus was saying the return is spiritual and not physical. John the Baptist was born of Elizabeth and Zachariah, had His own individual physical body, but enjoyed the same spiritual quality as Elias. Thus it was seen that "Return" is consigned to the return of the Spirit and not to the return of the physical body. The body of the returned Elias was that of John the Baptist.

The above description of the Son of man most likely does fit the appearance of Bahá'u'lláh. Following confinement in the dungeon known as the Síyáh-Chál, and in view of other difficulties that He faced, His hair had become *"white as snow."* In His own words:

> The cruelties inflicted by My oppressors, have bowed Me down, and turned My hair white.[19]

The *"One like unto the Son of man"* and characterized as He *"which is, and which was, and which is to come," "Alpha and Omega," "the beginning and the ending," "the Almighty," "a great voice, as of a trumpet,"* and *" the first and the last"* is Jesus Christ returned in the station of the "Father." He is manifested, made known, by Bahá'u'lláh Who carries the eternal spiritual qualities of God.

---

[19] Shoghi Effendi, *God Passes By,* Bahá'í Publishing Trust, Wilmette, Illinois, p. 169

As more fully developed throughout this commentary, it was Bahá'u'lláh, as the return of Jesus Christ, Who was *"in the midst of seven golden candlesticks"* or seven churches (1:20) that as previously discussed are understood to represent seven religions and their followers. *"[H]is voice [was] as the sound of many waters."* In station of the "Father" He comes with power and authority, and *"[H]e had in his right hand seven stars"* or *"angels of the seven churches,"* the Prophets (1:20). With the right hand of power He controls seven Prophets, and with *"[H]is voice as the sound of many waters"* He has inspired each of Them with the Word of God.

From His mouth went a sharp two-edged sword. The sword represents the Law of God. It has influence on people both within His institutions, the religions, and outside in the secular-political world. For this reason His sword is two-edged.

John Falls at His Feet

And when I saw him, I fell at his feet as dead. And he laid his right hand upon me, saying unto me, Fear not; I am the first and the last: I am he that liveth, and was dead; and, behold, I am alive for evermore, Amen; and have the keys of hell and of death. (17-18)

John falls at the feet of the Father but is told to fear not; the Father is *"the first and the last."* This same command is expressed in the following: (19:4-5, p. 181; 19:10, p. 183; and 22:8-9, p. 209). The Revelators, Prophets, or Manifestations are the way unto God!

The Father has eternal life, spirituality, and understands the true meaning (has keys) of this attribute of God. 'Abdu'l-Bahá who accompanied Bahá'u'lláh in banishment explains:

> Spirituality was my comfort, and turning to God was my greatest joy. If this had not been so, do you think it possible that I could have lived through those forty years in prison? Thus, spirituality is the greatest of God's gifts, and 'Life Everlasting' means 'Turning to God.'[20]

---

[20] 'Abdu'l-Bahá, *Paris Talks,* Bahá'í Publishing Trust, 27, Rutland Gate, London S.W. 7, p.112.

In numerous places, the scriptures speak of spiritual and physical death, as for example when Jesus came "down from heaven" though born of Mary, He is speaking of His spiritual life. (Jn 3:13, 6:33, 6:58, and 6:61)

Each of the Prophets, collectively the Lamb, has experienced physical death, and they now, as Spirits before His throne, have eternal life in the spiritual realm.

Create a Record

Write the things which thou hast seen, and the things which are, and the things which shall be hereafter; The mystery of the seven stars which thou sawest in my right hand, and the seven golden candlesticks. The seven stars are the angels of the seven churches: and the seven candlesticks which thou sawest are the seven churches. (19-20)

John is instructed to write what he has seen, the things that are, and things of the future (prophecy). His Book is for all religions so that all people of the world can participate in reordering that which is predestined for humanity.

The Father provides the metaphoric meaning of the *"seven stars"* and *"seven golden candlesticks:"* the *"seven stars are the angels [Prophets] of the seven churches"* and the *"seven golden candlesticks...are the seven churches"* (religions), and "angels" and "churches" remain metaphoric for further meaning as indicated by the previous discussion.

Revelation Chapters 2 and 3

About the Return

Reflecting on the subject of the "Return" of Jesus Christ in conjunction with some investigation of other religions indicates that "return of the Prophet" frames a concept shared among various religions. As noted in the previous chapter, the Book of Revelation is addressed to seven religions, and these would logically be those religions, like Christianity, that look for a time of fulfillment of their prophecies and of a time when the conditions of "last days" or "end times" will be fulfilled. Shoghi Effendi clarifies this matter of return as he explains the significance of the stations of the Báb and Bahá'u'lláh:

> He [the Báb], as affirmed by Himself, 'the Primal Point from which have been generated all created things,' 'one of the sustaining pillars of the Primal Word of God,' the 'Mystic Fane,' the 'Great Announcement,' the 'Flame of that supernal Light that glowed upon Sinai,' the 'Remembrance of God' concerning Whom 'a separate Covenant hath been established with each and every Prophet' had, through His advent, at once fulfilled the promise of all ages and ushered in the consummation of all Revelations. He the 'Qa'im' (He Who ariseth) promised to the Shí'ahs, the 'Mihdi' (One Who is guided) awaited by the Sunnis, the 'Return of John the Baptist' expected by the Christians, the 'Ushidar-Mah' referred to in the Zoroastrian scriptures, the 'Return of Elijah' anticipated by the Jews, Whose Revelation was to show forth 'the signs and tokens of all the Prophets', Who was to 'manifest the perfection of Moses, the radiance of Jesus and the patience of Job' had appeared, proclaimed His Cause, been mercilessly persecuted and died gloriously.[21]

---

[21] Shoghi Effendi, *God Passes By,* Bahá'í Publishing Trust, Wilmette, Illinois, pp. 57-58.

To Israel He [Bahá'u'lláh] was neither more nor less than the incarnation of the 'Everlasting Father,' the 'Lord of Hosts' come down 'with ten thousands of saints'; to Christendom Christ returned 'in the glory of the Father,' to Shi'ah Islam the return of the Imam Husayn; to Sunni Islam the descent of the 'Spirit of God' (Jesus Christ); to the Zoroastrians the promised Shah-Bahram; to the Hindus the reincarnation of Krishna; to the Buddhists the fifth Buddha.[22]

These quotations include reference to the Faith of Jews, Moses; Hindus, Krishna; Zoroastrians, Zoroaster; Buddhists, Buddha; Christians, Jesus Christ; and Muslims, Muhammad. The Sabean religion, because it is mentioned three times in the Old Testament and likely represents the basis of some early biblical commentary, possibly in the time frame of Abraham, is included within the same classification of religions. These are, then, the seven religions to which the Book of Revelation is addressed. It is also recognized that other religions exist, but the above selections appear to hold particular relevance to the message of the Book of Revelation.

In these two chapters each of the seven religions (churches) receive a letter. The letters generally present six messages that include: A) Identification of the speaker, B) Commendations, C) Condemnations, D) Admonitions, E) Encouragement for Spiritual Hearing, and F) Promised Rewards to those who overcome. The content of like categories among the seven religions is undoubtedly meaningful for the student of comparative religions, but the last category, representing clues to that which will transpire in the future, is of particular interest to most everyone and for this reason is presented in the following commentary.

Rewards for Those Who Overcome

To "overcome" is to find the Prophet, as relevant to the return of Jesus Christ, and hear His message at the time of His appearance and spiritual renewal. In this context while addressing Americans, 'Abdu'l-Bahá had stated:

---

[22] Ibid, p. 94

Now strive ye that the Collective Center of the sacred religions - for the inculcation of which all the Prophets were manifested and which is no other than the spirit of the divine teachings - be spread in all parts of America, so that each one of you may shine forth from the horizon of reality like unto the morning star, divine illumination may overcome the darkness of nature, and the world of humanity may become enlightened. This is the most great work! Should you become confirmed therein, this world will become another world, the surface of the earth will become the delectable paradise, and eternal Institutions be founded.[23]

Difficulties toward this end, as in the past, will exist. He will come in clouds of theological suppositions—initially be unseen by many. But ample rewards are promised for those who persevere and seek His return. The promises are presented in the following:

To him that overcometh...
   will I give to eat of the tree of life, which is in the midst of the paradise of God. 2:7

God's Prophet, from age to age, comes as "The tree of life [that] is the highest degree of the world of existence: the position of the Word of God, and the supreme Manifestation."[24] Through the teachings of the Prophet, who is also know as the Manifestation of God, the spirit of mankind is resurrected in each age. The Prophet of this age, promised by "return," will bring teachings for a global society that is compared to paradise.

To him that overcometh...
   shall not be hurt of the second death. 2:11

Those who are unable to recognize the birth of revelation are seen as being spiritually dead, (20:6). Those who were unable to recognize the

---

[23] 'Abdu'l-Bahá, *Tablets of the Divine Plan*, Bahá'í Publishing Trust, Wilmette, Illinois, p. 106
[24] 'Abdu'l-Bahá, *Some Answered Questions*, Bahá'í Publishing Trust, Wilmette, Illinois, p. 124.

Revelation of Jesus Christ suffered the first death. Those who miss the Revelation of this age will suffer the second death, but those who overcome do not experience this loss.

To him that overcometh...
will I give to eat of the hidden manna, and will give him a white stone, and in the stone a new name written, which no man knoweth saving he that receiveth it. 2:17

To those who overcome will be given manna, food from God that is spiritual and renewed with each new revelation, that is hidden to those who do not overpower their passiveness toward search. They who find God's message for this age will receive, also, a "new name" metaphorically noted as a *"white stone... [engraved with] a name written, which no man knoweth saving he that receiveth it."* Believers who subscribe to the spiritual qualities of renewal are identified with a new name.

The ancient Romans used a small tablet, known as tesserae, of wood, bone, or ivory as a means of identification. It was a four-cornered piece as used in mosaic work.[25]

To him that overcometh…
and keepeth my works unto the end, to him will I give power over the nations: And he shall rule them with a rod of iron; as the vessels of a potter shall they be broken to shivers: even as I received of my father. And I will give him the morning star. 2:26-28

A global civilization, p. 48, comprising a society in which war becomes obsolete is in need of spiritual values. Those who persevere through the difficult times of transformation from the old to the new world, a global society, and relate to the value system of the new order will have influence on the institutions of the world and on nations and their people. Each new revelation and renewal of religion brings the *"morning star."* It is the Prophet and light of a new day of God.

---

[25] *Webster's Third New International Dictionary.*

To him that overcometh...

the same shall be clothed in white raiment; and I will not blot out his name out of the book of life, but I will confess his name before my father, and before his angels. 3:5

White raiment is symbolic covering for those with spiritual values reinstated by renewal of religion. They retain their name in the *"book of life"* that is a metaphoric document for the followers of God's Cause renewed.

To him that overcometh...

will I make a pillar in the temple of my God, and he shall go no more out: and I will write upon him the name of my God, and the name of the city of my God, which is new Jerusalem, which cometh down out of heaven from my God: and I will write upon him my new name. 3:12

A New Jerusalem that encompasses the entire earth is the ultimate goal of the Book of Revelation; manifested as a religion, it brings the City of God and New Jerusalem. "We have before explained that what is most frequently meant by the Holy City, the Jerusalem of God, which is mentioned in the Holy Book, is the Law of God. It is compared sometimes to a bride, and sometimes to Jerusalem, and again to the new heaven and earth."[26] Spiritual qualities, inspired by God's anointed, the return of the Prophet, bring renewed teachings for a new age. Followers live in the name, or spirit, of spiritual renewal and take on a new organizational name; for example, followers of religion were previously known as Jew, Christian or Muslim.

To him that overcometh...

will I grant to sit with me in my throne, even as I also overcame, and am set down with my father in his throne. 3:21

Followers of renewed religion occupy the temple and throne of God's Cause with expressions of new teachings. In a physical sense these are buildings dedicated to shrines, administration and worship.

---

[26] 'Abdu'l-Bahá, *Some Answered Questions,* Bahá'í Publishing Trust, Wilmette, Illinois, p. 67.

Although the above verses are from Chapters 2 and 3, their meaning and path of fulfillment is more fully developed in the remaining 19-Chapters of the Book of Revelation. The content of the entire Book of Revelation is important to the churches, for its message becomes an invitation for them, followers of all religions, to participate in affairs of the future.

Revelation Chapter 4

The Father

After this I looked, and, behold, a door was opened in heaven: and the first voice which I heard was as it were of a trumpet talking with me; which said, Come up hither, and I will show thee things which must be hereafter. And immediately I was in the spirit; and, behold, a throne was set in heaven, and one sat on the throne. And he that sat was to look upon like jasper and a sardine stone: and there was a rainbow round about the throne, in sight like unto an emerald. (1-3)

John is now being introduced to what must be hereafter. The individuals and figures of this heavenly scene are to play an active earthly role of fulfillment at a later time. Prophecy originates in the spiritual world and predates historical events on earth.

God as an entity is *seen* in this heavenly view in the semblance of a person, as Prophet, who comes at the time of Jesus' return in the Station of the Father. He was identified by Verses 1:12-16. Jesus' appearance and spiritual qualities, as Father, are likened to a jasper and sardine stone. A rainbow around the throne, presented as an emerald, represents a spectrum of colors and symbolizes the reflection of all spiritual qualities. In Gen. 9:11-17 the rainbow was made the symbol of God's covenant; it is central to the teachings of all the Prophets, and in this age the "Father" continues with the covenant in His capacity as the "Lord of Hosts."

> When Bahá'u'lláh came to this prison in the Holy Land, the wise men realized that the glad tidings which God gave through the tongue of the Prophets two or three thousand years before were again manifested, and that God was faithful to His promise; for to some of the Prophets He had revealed and given the good news that 'the Lord of Hosts should be manifested in the Holy Land.' [27]

---

[27] 'Abdu'l-Bahá, *Some Answered Questions,* Bahá'í Publishing Trust, Wilmette, Illinois. P. 32.

The Elders

And round about the throne were four and twenty seats: and upon the seats I saw four and twenty elders sitting, clothed in white raiment; and they had on their heads crowns of gold. (4)

Twenty-four elders sit round about the throne and wear *"white raiment"* of righteousness and *"crowns of gold"* of spiritual authority. The elders, known as Letters of the Living, represent the first recipients of new revelation, and can be compared to the disciples of Jesus Christ.

> Regarding the four and twenty elders: The Master ['Abdu'l-Bahá], in a Tablet, stated that they were the Báb, the eighteen Letters of the Living, and five others who would be known in the future. So far we do not know who these five others are.[28]

The reason for having 24 elders is explained on p. 116.

Seven Lamps of Fire

And out of the throne proceeded lightnings and thunderings and voices: and there were seven lamps of fire burning before the throne, which are the seven Spirits of God. (5)

Authority and might of the throne is seen and heard by John as *"lightnings, and thunderings and voices."* These occurrences signify revelation that reverberates in a clash of social change. Every Moses and Jesus proclaims His message, lifts-up His followers, and is cause for a paradigm shift in social evolution.

"Seven lamps of fire...before the throne" of the Father, signify *"seven Spirits of God"* who are the angels (Prophets) of the seven churches (Religions), and noted as *"seven Spirits before his throne."* See also v. 5:6 p. 64. These Prophets speak for God, are endowed with His Spirit, and have taken His Cause throughout the earth.

Friendly Beasts

And before the throne there was a sea of glass like unto crystal: and in the midst of the throne, and round about the throne, were four beasts full of eyes before and behind. And the

---

[28] Gertrude Garrida, *Directives From The Guardian,* Bahá'í Publishing Trust, New Delhi, India, p 22.

first beast was like a lion, and the second beast like a calf, and the third beast had a face as a man, and the fourth beast was like a flying eagle. And the four beasts had each of them six wings about him; and they were full of eyes within: and they rest not day and night, saying, Holy, holy, holy, Lord God Almighty, which was, and is, and is to come. (6-8)

The floor before the throne, likened to a *"sea of glass like unto crystal,"* betokens the firm, hard and smooth foundation of understanding on which its occupants stand. Four beasts in the midst and around the throne are friends of God's Cause as shown by their praise of Lord God Almighty, *"Holy, holy, holy, Lord God Almighty, which was, and is, and is to come."*

The symbolism of Revelation uses both friendly and unfriendly beasts. Friendly beasts of great insight (eyes within) stand on firm spiritual footing, while their unfriendly counter parts, as noted later, are without spiritual development.

These friendly beasts may represent political or secular leaders. They possess spiritual qualities without which mankind merely exemplifies the temperament of a beast. Attaining to spirituality, man's qualities tend toward the angelic. These friendly beasts appear in Chapters 4, 5, 6, 7, 14, 15 and 19. In addition to their great insight and foreknowledge, they provide continuing service to the Cause of God and praise unto God upon the throne.

Beasts Worship Father

And when those beasts give glory and honour and thanks to him that sat on the throne, who liveth for ever and ever, The four and twenty elders fall down before him that sat on the throne, and worship him that liveth for ever and ever, and cast their crowns before the throne, saying, Thou art worthy, O Lord, to receive glory and honour and power: for thou hast created all things, and for thy pleasure they are and were created. (9-11)

Twenty-four elders *"cast their crowns before the throne"* when the beasts gives praise unto the Father. It is especially significant that the beasts, as possible political or secular leaders, give praise to God. Could it be that the elders, as faithful followers, are pleased to see the participation of the beasts and are willing to share their quality of servitude by casting their crowns before the throne?

The elders announce a general concept that is fundamental to religion and basic to understanding spiritual progress. God has created all things for His pleasure and is worthy to receive glory, honor, and power.

Movement toward a new heaven and new earth, the renewed Law of God as later explained, is concurrent with increasing maturity and spirituality of mankind. God's pleasure, as revealed by the Book of Revelation, enjoins mankind to reflect heavenly qualities in social transactions; God's glory, honor, and power will be apparent when humanity attains to this spiritual level of conduct.

Revelation Chapter 5

The Book

And I saw in the right hand of him that sat on the throne a book written within and on the backside, sealed with seven seals. (1)

The Occupant of the throne, Who John sees, is He who was in the midst of the seven candlesticks (1:12:16, p. 48) and designated as the Father.

The book in His *"right hand"* has been filled, overflows on the backside, and remains sealed. Past Revelations and their subsequent controversial theologies have been sealed (not fully disclosed) following the passing of their respective Prophets; that is why interpretation of texts has been attempted through theology and philosophy which fact may account for the writings on the backside. Much speculation concerning last things has been written, but the process of religion and its continuity has never been fully understood. Writings on the back side also suggest there is more information to come. Preliminaries to revealing the mystery of religions and their future will be disclosed by opening the seven seals of the Father's Book.

Who is Worthy to Open the Book?

And I saw a strong angel proclaiming with a loud voice, Who is worthy to open the book, and to loose the seals thereof? And no man in heaven, nor in earth, neither under the earth, was able to open the book, neither to look thereon. And I wept much, because no man was found worthy to open and to read the book, neither to look thereon. (2-4)

An angel with great spiritual strength and firm voice states an important question — *"who is worthy to open the book"* and disclose its content? John weeps when he sees that no man is able or found *"worthy to open and read the book."* Man, without enlightenment from the Spirit, cannot accomplish this task! Only God knows the outcome of humanity's future as revealed to the Prophets.

The Lamb and Seven Spirits of God

And one of the elders saith unto me, Weep not: behold, the Lion of the tribe of Juda, the Root of David, hath prevailed to open the book, and to loose the seven seals thereof. And I beheld, and, lo, in the midst of the throne and of the four beasts, and in the midst of the elders, stood a Lamb as it had been slain, having seven horns and seven eyes, which are the seven Spirits of God sent forth into all the earth. (5-6)

An elder, p. 60, from the period of the second woe, p. 21, explains to John that *"the Lion of the tribe of Juda,"* a relative of David, has prevailed to open the book. He will *"loose the seven seals."* Symbolized as a Lamb, *"as it had been slain,"* He stands in the *"midst of the throne,"* the beasts, and the elders and has seven horns and seven eyes that exemplify *"seven Spirits of God."* His multiple qualities, personified by the *"seven Spirits of God,"* allude to the unity of the Prophets. All come down from heaven, even as Jesus came *"down from heaven"* though He was born of Mary, p. 50.

Prophets have all suffered persecution and rejection by the vested powers of their time, and for this reason are likened unto a lamb because of its sacrificial qualities. Numerous Prophets, in this instance the seven Spirits of God, have been *"sent forth into all the earth."* They have the quality of seven stars (1:12-16, p. 48), of seven lamps of fire (4:5, p. 60), and of seven eyes (5:6, p. 64). Stars, lamps, and eyes all carry the imagery of light and delivery of the Word of God. The Lamb has seven horns that are the names of the major Revelators (Spirits) as presented in Chapters 2 and 3, p. 54.

Although the Book of Revelation places emphasis on seven specific appearances of the Lamb as addressees of the message of the Book of Revelation and Founders of as many religions, the designation of Lamb, appropriate to all Prophets, is also used in referring to Bahá'u'lláh and the Báb.

The Lamb Takes the Book

And he came and took the book out of the right hand of him that sat upon the throne. (7)

The Lamb takes the book out of the right hand of the Eternal Father who sat on the throne. This is the scene, but it is the Father as dicussed below, who will open the book.

The forerunner of Bahá'u'lláh, the Báb, persecuted by the Powers of Persia was put to death by a regiment of 750 riflemen, and received the station of Martyrdom. He *"stood a Lamb as it had been slain."* The Báb closed the Cycle of Prophecy and initiated the Cycle of Fulfillment as opened and championed by Bahá'u'lláh. The Báb, as attested by His own words, received His power from Bahá'u'lláh:

> 'Today the Bayan [the Báb's Holy Book] is in the stage of seed; at the beginning of the manifestation of Him Whom God shall make manifest [Bahá'u'lláh] its ultimate perfection will become apparent.' 'The Bayan deriveth all its glory from Him Whom God shall make manifest.' 'All that hath been revealed in the Bayan is but a ring upon My hand, and I Myself am, verily, but a ring upon the hand of Him Whom God shall make manifest... He turneth it as He pleaseth, for whatsoever He pleaseth, and through whatsoever He pleaseth. He, verily, is the Help in Peril, the Most High.'[29]

The following verses, Isaiah, 11:1-10, are generally considered by Christian commentators as being applicable to the first advent of Jesus Christ.[30] 'Abdu'l-Bahá refers to these same verses to explain Bahá'u'lláh's station in relation to the "Lion of the tribe of Juda, The Root of David." Jesse is the root of David.

> And there shall come forth a rod out of the stem of Jesse, and a Branch shall grow out of his roots: And the spirit of the Lord shall rest upon him, the spirit of wisdom and understanding, the spirit of counsel and might, the spirit of knowledge and of the fear of the Lord; And shall make him of quick understanding in the fear of the Lord: and he shall not judge after the sight of his eyes, neither reprove after the hearing of his ears: But with righteousness shall he judge the poor, and reprove with equity for the meek of the earth: and he shall smite the earth with the rod of his mouth, and with the breath of his lips shall he slay the wicked.

---

[29] Shoghi Effendi, *God Passes By,* Bahá'í Publishing Trust, Wilmette, Illinois, p. 30.
[30] *Unger's Bible Dictionary*

And righteousness shall be the girdle of his loins, and faithfulness the girdle of his reins. The wolf also shall dwell with the lamb, and the leopard shall lie down with the kid; and the calf and the young lion and the fatling together; and a little child shall lead them. And the cow and the bear shall feed; their young ones shall lie down together: and the lion shall eat straw like the ox. And the sucking child shall play on the hole of the asp, and the weaned child shall put his hand on the cockatrice' den. They shall not hurt nor destroy in all My holy mountain: for the earth shall be full of the knowledge of the Lord, as the waters cover the sea. (Isa 11:1-10)

This rod out of the stem of Jesse might be correctly applied to Christ, for Joseph was of the descendants of Jesse, the father of David; but as Christ found existence through the Spirit of God, He called Himself the Son of God. If He had not done so, this description would refer to Him. Besides this, the events which he indicated as coming to pass in the days of that rod, if interpreted symbolically, were in part fulfilled in the day of Christ, but not all; and if not interpreted, then decidedly none of these signs happened. For example, the leopard and the lamb, the lion and the calf, the child and the asp, are metaphors and symbols for various nations, peoples, antagonistic sects and hostile races, who are as opposite and inimical as the wolf and lamb. We say that by the breath of the spirit of Christ they found concord and harmony, they were vivified, and they associated together.

But 'they shall not hurt nor destroy in all My holy mountain: for the earth shall be full of the knowledge of the Lord, as the waters cover the sea.' These conditions did not prevail in the time of the manifestation of Christ; for until today various and antagonistic nations exist in the world: very few acknowledge the God of Israel, and the greater number are without the knowledge of God. In the same way, universal peace did not come into existence in the time of Christ - that is to say, between the antagonistic and hostile nations there was neither peace nor concord, disputes and disagreements did not cease, and reconciliation and sincerity did not appear. So, even at this day, among the Christian sects and nations themselves, enmity, hatred and the most violent hostility are met with.

But these verses apply word for word to Bahá'u'lláh. Likewise in this marvelous cycle the earth will be transformed, and the world of humanity arrayed in tranquility and beauty. Disputes, quarrels and murders will be replaced by peace, truth and concord; among the nations, peoples, races and countries, love and amity will appear. Cooperation and union will be established, and finally war will be entirely suppressed. When the laws of the Most Holy Book are enforced, contentions and disputes will find a final sentence of absolute justice before a general tribunal of the nations and kingdoms, and the difficulties that appear will be solved. The five continents of the world will form but one, the numerous nations will become one, the surface of the earth will become one land, and mankind will be a single community. The relations between the countries - the mingling, union and friendship of the peoples and communities - will reach to such a degree that the human race will be like one family and kindred. The light of heavenly love will shine, and the darkness of enmity and hatred will be dispelled from the world. Universal peace will raise its tent in the center of the earth, and the blessed Tree of Life will grow and spread to such an extent that it will overshadow the East and the West. Strong and weak, rich and poor, antagonistic sects and hostile nations - which are like the wolf and the lamb, the leopard and kid, the lion and the calf - will act toward each other with the most complete love, friendship, justice and equity. The world will be filled with science, with the knowledge of the reality of the mysteries of beings, and with the knowledge of God.

Now consider, in this great century which is the cycle of Bahá'u'lláh, what progress science and knowledge have made, how many secrets of existence have been discovered, how many great inventions have been brought to light and are day by day multiplying in number. Before long, material science and learning, as well as the knowledge of God, will make such progress and will show forth such wonders that the beholders will be amazed. Then the mystery of this verse in Isaiah, 'For the earth shall be full of the knowledge of the Lord,' will be completely evident.

Reflect also that in the short time since Bahá'u'lláh has appeared, people from all countries, nations and races have entered under the shadow of this Cause. Christians, Jews, Zoroastrians, Buddhists, Hindus and Persians all associate together with the greatest friendship and love, as if indeed these people had been related and connected together, they and theirs, for a thousand years; for they are like father and child, mother and daughter, sister and brother. This is one of the meanings of the companionship of the wolf and the lamb, the leopard and the kid, and the lion and the calf.

One of the great events which is to occur in the Day of the manifestation of that Incomparable Branch (Bahá'u'lláh) is the hoisting of the Standard of God among all nations. By this is meant that all nations and kindreds will be gathered together under the shadow of this Divine Banner, which is no other than the Lordly Branch itself, and will become a single nation. Religious and sectarian antagonism, the hostility of races and peoples, and differences among nations, will be eliminated. All men will adhere to one religion, will have one common faith, will be blended into one race, and become a single people. All will dwell in one common fatherland, which is the planet itself. Universal peace and concord will be realized between all the nations, and that Incomparable Branch will gather together all Israel, signifying that in this cycle Israel will be gathered in the Holy Land, and that the Jewish people who are scattered to the East and West, South and North, will be assembled together.

Now see: these events did not take place in the Christian cycle, for the nations did not come under the One Standard, which is the Divine Branch. But in this cycle of the Lord of Hosts all the nations and peoples will enter under the shadow of this Flag. In the same way, Israel, scattered all over the world, was not reassembled in the Holy Land in the Christian cycle; but in the beginning of the cycle of Bahá'u'lláh this divine promise, as is clearly stated in all the Books of the Prophets, has begun to be manifest. You can see that from all the parts of the world tribes of Jews are coming to the Holy Land; they live in villages and lands which they make their own, and day by day they are increasing to such an extent that all Palestine will become their home.[31]

Beasts and Elders Sing a New Song

And when he had taken the book, the four beasts and four and twenty elders fell down before the Lamb, having every one of them harps, and golden vials full of odours, which are the prayers of saints. And they sung a new song, saying, Thou art worthy to take the book, and to open the seals thereof: for thou wast slain, and hast redeemed us to God by thy blood out of every kindred, and tongue, and people, and nation; And hast made us unto our God kings and priests: and we shall reign on the earth. (8-10)

The faithful supporters of the throne and followers of the Lamb, His immediate followers and apostles, are saints; they prayed for humanity as the future holds many difficulties. The *"four and twenty elders,"* as previously explained, are comparable to the disciples of Jesus Christ, and known as Letters of the Living.

The beasts and elders sing, understand and proclaim, the song of a new revelation that will be initiated at the time of the Báb's revelation. They participate in spiritual renewal and work to alleviate social depravity.

The Lamb, as Prophet, is *"worthy to take the book, and to open the seals thereof: for thou wast slain"* as explained following 5:7. Historically, the Lamb has been slain or persecuted and his prophetic function has redeemed peoples from every kindred, tongue, and nation.

The Lamb makes the champions of God's Cause kings and priests as noted in 1:6. Their new song, new teachings, shall be responsible for inspiring many peoples of the world.

---

[31] 'Abdu'l-Bahá, *Some Answered Questions,* Bahá'í Publishing Trust, Wilmette, Illinois, pp. 62-66.

Millions of Angels Join In

And I beheld, and I heard the voice of many angels round about the throne and the beasts and the elders: and the number of them was ten thousand times ten thousand, and thousands of thousands; Saying with a loud voice, Worthy is the Lamb that was slain to receive power, and riches, and wisdom, and strength, and honour, and glory, and blessing. (11-12)

John sees millions of angels, supported by the beasts and the elders, representing followers of the renewed throne of authority at the time of Jesus' return. The Book of Revelation brings the testimony of Jesus Christ (1:9, 19:10). The new song brings teachings for the promised city of God, which is New Jerusalem. These verses preview historical events, which culminate in a new City, a new heaven and a new earth.

Praise for the Throne and the Lamb

And every creature which is in heaven, and on the earth, and under the earth, and such as are in the sea, and all that are in them, heard I saying, Blessing, and honour, and glory, and power, be unto him that sitteth upon the throne, and unto the Lamb for ever and ever. And the four beasts said, Amen. And the four and twenty elders fell down and worshipped him that liveth for ever and ever. (13-14)

John now sees the significance of the messages to the churches, Chapters 2 and 3, and of the life to come! Now he understands the meaning of *"glory, and power, be unto him that sitteth upon the throne, and unto the Lamb"* and the potential for having a spiritual humanity in the distant future as measured from his time. All creatures heard John praise Bahá'u'lláh and His Forerunner, the Báb. They and Their immediate followers bring spiritual renewal in fulfillment of the promised return of Jesus Christ.

The Problem
And the Solution

Chapter 6

What "oppression" is more grievous than that a soul seeking the truth, and wishing to attain unto the knowledge of God, should know not where to go for it and from whom to seek it? For opinions have sorely differed, and the ways unto the attainment of God have multiplied. This "oppression" is the essential feature of every Revelation. Unless it cometh to pass, the Sun of Truth will not be made manifest. For the break of the morn of divine guidance must needs follow the darkness of the night of error. For this reason, in all chronicles and traditions reference hath been made unto these things, namely that iniquity shall cover the surface of the earth and darkness shall envelop mankind.

The Kitab-i-Iqan, pp. 31-32

Revelation Chapter 6

Social Environment

And I saw when the Lamb opened one of the seals, and I heard, as it were the noise of thunder, one of the four beasts saying, Come and see. And I saw, and behold a white horse: and he that sat on him had a bow; and a crown was given unto him: and he went forth conquering, and to conquer. (1-2)

As the Lamb opens one of the seals, John hears a voice of one of the four beasts saying, with the *"noise of thunder"* that likely portends a social storm, come and see. John sees a conquering horseman wearing a crown, carrying a bow, and riding a white horse. White is the color of purity and a crown signifies distinction or authority, so that the horse and its rider represent conquest in the name of religion. Spiritual conquest of an immature humanity has had limited success; religions have lacked arrows of attainment[32] and behavior of the populous falls short of spiritual ideals.

This rider and the three remaining horsemen reveal elements of the social environment that foresee a need for change so that the goals of the Book of Revelation can be enacted. As each of the first four seals is broken, one of the friendly beasts invites John to come and see. The friendly beasts, having keen awareness, are concerned about the human condition. Without the support of key social leaders, it would be difficult to make required changes. One is reminded of the support given to early Christianity by Constantine.

And when he had opened the second seal, I heard the second beast say, Come and see. And there went out another horse that was red: and power was given to him that sat thereon to take peace from the earth, and that they should kill one another: and there was given unto him a great sword. (3-4)

---

[32] Ruth J. Moffett, *New Keys to the Book of Revelation,* Bahá'í Publishing Trust, New Delhi 110024, p. 26.

On a red horse, the second rider is given the *"great sword"* of warfare and power *"to take peace from the earth."* In the struggling age of economic, political and religious development there exists throughout the centuries much warfare. With the irresponsibility of its youth, mankind takes with force the civilizations and resources of the earth. Now a crisis of survival exists among the competing nations of the world. With the advent of atomic energy the atmosphere of the whole earth can be poisoned; the potential for a nuclear winter and the need for retention of sanity among nations makes of warfare a non-operative condition.

And when he had opened the third seal, I heard the third beast say, Come and see. And I beheld, and lo a black horse; and he that sat on him had a pair of balances in his hand. And I heard a voice in the midst of the four beasts say, A measure of wheat for a penny, and three measures of barley for a penny; and see thou hurt not the oil and the wine. (5-6)

Next, John sees a black horse whose rider carries the scales of economic justice. An evaluation of material wealth finds the distribution out of balance. *"Hurt not the oil and the wine."* These are luxury items and, by all means, should be protected.

Present commercial use of oil, undoubtedly the largest drain of natural resources, is being used at an unsustainable rate. It raises the issues of judicious use of the earth's material wealth, of preservation of life in the wake of conquest of nature, and of the effort to maximize profit without responsibility for conservation.

And when he had opened the fourth seal, I heard the voice of the fourth beast say, Come and see. And I looked, and behold a pale horse: and his name that sat on him was Death, and Hell followed with him. And power was given unto them over the fourth part of the earth, to kill with sword, and with hunger, and with death, and with the beasts of the earth. (7-8)

With opening of the fourth seal, John sees a pale horse whose rider is spiritually dead; *"Hell followed with him."* The developments of civilization in most parts of the world have seen many pitfalls. This horse and rider signify the power of social warfare and the accentuated need for material goods, a condition mostly out of balance and controlled by ambitious worldly beasts. In this respect, religious and political leaders in the conduct of social affairs are not always able to live up to the high standards befitting their station as role models. They then assume the qualities of the beasts of the earth whose behavior draw out the values of *"Death and Hell."*

History shows that European regions have experienced centuries of difficulty and are likely the domain referenced as the *"fourth part of the earth."* The Christian faith within this region, engaged in an internal power struggle with both religion and politics, remained the primary source of spiritual progress within its boundaries, became antagonistic to Islam, and in many instances compromised the sanctity of its spiritual purpose. Many leaders have exhausted their luster in the battle between religious and political control and could easily qualify as the symbolic rider of the pale horse.

The four horsemen symbolize social environments occupied with war and conquest, in need of compassion and justice, and manifesting social indifference. These characteristics, John sees, can lead only to a future in need of social change. A modern view from within the new millennium sees the present inequitable distribution of both spiritual values and material needs as a universal situation. The goals of the Book of Revelation require many social adjustments, universally applied, for the making of a spiritual environment.

Past Martyrs

And when he had opened the fifth seal, I saw under the altar the souls of them that were slain for the word of God, and for the testimony which they held: And they cried with a loud voice, saying, How long, O Lord, holy and true, dost thou not judge and avenge our blood on them that dwell on the earth? (9-10)

The opening of the fifth seal exposes many martyrs who had worked for God's Cause in the past. History is replete with religious persecutions as at the birth of Christianity. Revelation and religious renewal, the means for fostering social improvement, has always suffered at the hands of vested powers. Past martyrs are impatient and want the Lord to *"judge and avenge their blood"* because of the wrongs committed against them while in the service of God's Cause. These spiritual heroes are close to God under the protection of the altar. They ask, *"How long, O Lord, holy and true, dost thou not judge and avenge our blood on them that dwell on the earth?"*

And white robes were given unto every one of them; and it was said unto them, that they should rest yet for a little season, until their fellowservants also and their brethren, that should be killed as they were, should be fulfilled. (11)

The cost of renewing the Law of God, its content of sacrifice, is acknowledged. Martyrs from past religious renewals were recognized and given white robes of righteousness, p. 57, and told they must wait *"until their fellowservants also and their brethren, that should be killed as they were, should be fulfilled."* Sacrifice occurs at a time of spiritual renewal when God does judge and avenge the blood of the past. This verse foreshadows the time when social issues as suggested by the four horsemen shall be resolved, and the human spirit through the vehicle of religion is renewed.

A Great Earthquake

And I beheld when he had opened the sixth seal, and, lo, there was a great earthquake; and the sun became black as sackcloth of hair, and the moon became as blood; (12)

The sixth seal foresees the coming storm and earthquake of adjustment that comes with spiritual renewal. At times of revelation the social environment is destined for drastic changes, and it can be seen that the sun, the symbol of spiritual light, is darkened because past teachings have lost their savor. Religion becomes old as sackcloth, and its moon of spiritual reflection has deceased; institutions become as the spirit of a dead man. These conditions are the norm of "last days" of a religious dispensation.

Nothing on earth can be demonstrated by words alone, and every level of existence is known by its signs and symbols, and every degree in man's development has its identifying mark. [33]

---

[33] 'Abdu'l-Bahá, *Secret of Divine Civilization,* National Spiritual Assembly of the Bahá'ís of the United States, p. 98-99.

And the stars of heaven fell unto the earth, even as a fig tree casteth her untimellly figs, when she is shaken of a mighty wind. And the heaven departed as a scroll when it is rolled together; and every mountain and island were moved out of their places. (13-14)

At "end times" stars of heaven, religious leaders, fall from power and the heaven of divine understanding vanishes as with a closed book. Bahá'u'lláh explains:

> Hence, it is clear and manifest that by the words 'the sun shall be darkened, and the moon shall not give her light, and the stars shall fall from heaven' is intended the waywardness of the divines, and the annulment of laws firmly established by divine Revelation, all of which, in symbolic language, have been foreshadowed by the Manifestation of God.[34]

Institutional sanctuaries, likened to mountains and islands, forfeit their authority as witnessed by the many divisions of contemporary religions. Vested powers of tradition relinquish their supremacy when the social order is advanced by the workings of renewal. The Book of Revelation is about God's plan for worldwide spiritual redemption.

All Men Fear God

And the kings of the earth, and the great men, and the rich men, and the chief captains, and the mighty men, and every bondman, and every free man, hid themselves in the dens and in the rocks of the mountains; And said to the mountains and rocks, Fall on us, and hide us from the face of him that sitteth on the throne, and from the wrath of the Lamb: For the great day of his wrath is come; and who shall be able to stand? (15-17)

Mighty men whatever their position, of the old order, become concerned because the Father and His Lamb shall take power. They hide for safety in the rock and mountain like sanctuaries of past institutions. Who shall be able to stand in the great day of wrath, that time of transition

---

[34] Bahá'u'lláh, *Kitáb-i-Íqán*, Bahá'í Publishing Trust, Wilmette, Illinois, p. 41.

from the old order of regionalism to the new heaven and new earth of wider understanding, the early phase of a global society? The scene is reminiscent of Jewish difficulties under the Romans at the birth of Christianity except that now the difficulties operate at a global level.

God has created all things for His pleasure (4:11, p. 61) and conditions bring Him pleasure when the quality of life for humankind become spiritually oriented—this, at a global level, is the ultimate earthly goal anticipated by the Book of Revelation.

Preparation

Chapter 7

In like manner, endeavour to comprehend the meaning of the "changing of the earth." Know thou, that upon whatever hearts the bountiful showers of mercy, raining from the "heaven" of divine Revelation, have fallen, the earth of those hearts hath verily been changed into the earth of divine knowledge and wisdom. What myrtles of unity hath the soil of their hearts produced! What blossoms of true knowledge and wisdom hath their illumined bosoms yielded!

The Kitáb-I-Íqán, p. 46

Revelation Chapter 7

Hold the Four Winds of Change

And after these things I saw four angels standing on the four corners of the earth, holding the four winds of the earth, that the wind should not blow on the earth, nor on the sea, nor on any tree. And I saw another angel ascending from the east, having the seal of the living God: and he cried with a loud voice to the four angels, to whom it was given to hurt the earth and the sea, Saying, Hurt not the earth, neither the sea, nor the trees, till we have sealed the servants of our God in their foreheads. (1-3)

The heavenly vision continues as John sees four angels with power to hold back the winds of change from over the whole earth. The earth, sea and trees, symbols of spiritual understanding and its source, should not be adjusted at this time. These life forms consist of organic systems. The ultimate life form, the Tree of Life, is rooted in the earth of spiritual understanding and signifies the Prophet of God.[35]

> This tree of life was the position of the Reality of Christ; through His manifestation it was planted and adorned with everlasting fruits.[36]

John sees another angel from the east having credentials from God and holding commanding power over the angels of the wind. He orders the angels of the wind to change not the earth and sea of human understanding until the word of new revelation confirms the servants of God. Adequate preparation is essential for success of renewal.

The Prophet causes consciousness of the Law of God to grow from out of the soil of the human heart, and new awareness restores a living spirit.

---

[35] 'Abdu'l-Bahá, *Some Answered Questions,* Bahá'í Publishing Trust, Wilmette, Illinois, p. 124.
[36] Ibid

Revelation brings a sea (reservoir) of direction enumerated by the Word of God and from the waters of guidance individuals and living institutions experience transformation.

The winds of change, which must appear because of the abused environment of the horsemen, shall sweep the earth, but activity directed toward renewal of the human spirit is held in abeyance until the appropriate time. The storm of change will subside as humanity gains greater understanding.

Children Advance Spiritually

And I heard the number of them which were sealed: and there were sealed an hundred and forty and four thousand of all the tribes of the children of Israel. Of the tribe of Juda were sealed twelve thousand. Of the tribe of Reuben were sealed twelve thousand. Of the tribe of Gad were sealed twelve thousand. Of the tribe of Aser were sealed twelve thousand. Of the tribe of Nephthalim were sealed twelve thousand. Of the tribe of Manasses were sealed twelve thousand. Of the tribe of Simeon were sealed twelve thousand. Of the tribe of Levi were sealed twelve thousand. Of the tribe of Issachar were sealed twelve thousand. Of the tribe of Zabulon were sealed twelve thousand. Of the tribe of Joseph were sealed twelve thousand. Of the tribe of Benjamin were sealed twelve thousand. (4-8)

Twelve thousand persons from each of the twelve *"tribes of the children of Israel"* are confirmed in spiritual awareness and understanding and thereby sealed. Spiritual development and insight is enhanced with renewal of religion. Could it be that they are referenced as *"children"* because of limited spiritual development and are now being raised to spiritual maturity? That they are from each of the twelve tribes of Israel represents unity and completeness of God's Cause in preparation for universal participation. Ten of the tribes were lost to history following conquest of Israel. Inclusion of their scattered remnants becomes symbolic of an alliance of all peoples. God's plan for this age is all encompassing.

A Multitude Worship God

After this I beheld, and, lo, a great multitude, which no man could number, of all nations, and kindreds, and people, and tongues, stood before the throne, and before the Lamb, clothed with white robes, and palms in their hands; And cried with a loud voice, saying, Salvation to our God which sitteth upon the throne, and unto the Lamb. And all the an-

gels stood round about the throne, and about the elders and the four beasts, and fell before the throne on their faces, and worshipped God, Saying, Amen: Blessing, and glory, and wisdom, and thanksgiving, and honour, and power, and might, be unto our God for ever and ever. Amen. (9-12)

John foresees great progress following the sealing of the servants. A multitude of new followers, beyond count, from all nations and tongues stood before the throne. They are clothed in white robes of purity, hold in their hands the trophy of righteousness, and offer praise and worship to God and the Lamb.

In Verses 5:11-12, p. 69, the Lamb is given power, and now he has gained a vast spiritual following that will support Him on the day of wrath; a time at which the new order begins to blossom and the old order works toward its own destruction.

Out of Great Tribulation

And one of the elders answered, saying unto me, What are these which are arrayed in white robes? and whence came they? And I said unto him, Sir, thou knowest. And he said to me, These are they which came out of great tribulation, and have washed their robes, and made them white in the blood of the Lamb. (13-14).

"What are these which are arrayed in white robes? and whence came they?" One of the elders explained that the multitude around the throne, and the elders and beasts are from the great tribulation that accompanies the second and third Woes, p. 21, and is a time of new revelation. These persons are servants and followers who participate in the coming age of spiritual renewal. They retain the Spirit of the Lamb, and many of them have suffered or become martyrs for His cause.

Living Fountains of Water

Therefore are they before the throne of God, and serve him day and night in his temple: and he that sitteth on the throne shall dwell among them. They shall hunger no more, neither thirst any more; neither shall the sun light on them, nor any heat. For the Lamb which is in the midst of the throne shall feed them, and shall lead them unto living fountains of waters: and God shall wipe away all tears from their eyes. (15-17)

God on the throne *"shall wipe away all tears from their eyes,"* and the Lamb in the midst of the throne shall *"feed them"* with new holy verses. The Prophets carry the function of Divine Educators, remove the sorrow of the multitude and guide the followers in spiritual development. They lead the followers unto the living waters of renewal and thereby wipe away all tears of unrighteousness.

There is no doubt that the purpose of a divine law is the education of the human race, the training of humanity. All mankind may be considered as pupils or children who are in need of a divine Educator, a real Teacher.[37]

---

[37] 'Abdu'l-Bahá, *Promulgation of Universal Peace,* Bahá'í Publishing Trust, Wilmette, Illinois, p. 406

Trumpets of History

Chapters 8 and 9

And now concerning thy question regarding the nature of religion. Know thou that they who are truly wise have likened the world unto the human temple. As the body of man needeth a garment to clothe it, so the body of mankind must needs be adorned with the mantle of justice and wisdom. Its robe is the Revelation vouchsafed unto it by God. Whenever this robe hath fulfilled its purpose, the Almighty will assuredly renew it. For every age requireth a fresh measure of the light of God. Every Divine Revelation hath been sent down in a manner that befitted the circumstances of the age in which it hath appeared.

Gleanings, p. 81

Revelation Chapter 8

Trumpets of History

And when he had opened the seventh seal, there was silence in heaven about the space of half an hour. And I saw the seven angels which stood before God; and to them were given seven trumpets. (1-2)

Removal of the seventh seal, giving clearer vision of God's Cause and plans for the future, is reason for a brief period of overwhelming silence in heaven. Seven angels standing before the throne of the Father are given trumpets and commissioned to signal the pathway of history leading to the goals of the Book of Revelation. The angels will point to some difficulties of early Christianity and of three periods of woe of a later time. From this age we look backward to these events, but some sweeping social changes remain as unfinished business even on into the beginning of the third millennium since the revelation of Saint John.

And another angel came and stood at the altar, having a golden censer; and there was given unto him much incense, that he should offer it with the prayers of all saints upon the golden altar which was before the throne. And the smoke of the incense, which came with the prayers of the saints, ascended up before God out of the angel's hand. (3-4)

The *affairs of history* are working toward a new heaven and new earth, which will be recognized as a City that descends from heaven and sustains an overlay of spiritual enlightenment for the entire world—the Law of God renewed. *"All saints,"* those who work for God's Cause, as seen in previous chapters, pray for the successful attainment of this historic goal. Their prayers with the aroma of incense burned in a golden censer are as the odors of saints, (5:8), and offered to the throne by the angel.

And the angel took the censer, and filled it with fire of the altar, and cast it into the earth: and there were voices, and thunderings, and lightnings, and an earthquake. (5)

An angel cast into the earth the fire of the love of God. This action possessed sufficient energy to cause an earthquake, which is notable for its power to shake-up a present arrangement and lead to new understanding. In social systems, the old order may be replaced by a new paradigm. *"Voices," "thunderings,"* and *"lightnings"* are characteristic of a storm, which can be associated with an earthquake and suggest the fear of the beholders and of the power deployed to make for replacement of past social connections.

The social environment is reordered to adjust and compensate for a recession of spiritual behavior, a condition that exists at the end of a religious dispensation and occurs when humankind strays from its past values. The Law of God renewed by the Prophet leads to a higher level of spiritual consciousness.

First Four Angels and Christian History

And the seven angels which had the seven trumpets prepared themselves to sound. The first angel sounded, and there followed hail and fire mingled with blood, and they were cast upon the earth: and the third part of trees was burnt up, and all green grass was burnt up. (6-7)

Seven angels, each with a trumpet, shall sound, with emphasis, a direction of change. Following the sound of the first trumpet, hail and fire of Christian proclamation, mingled with blood of persecution was cast upon the human condition where it caused a shake-up in the ground of past learning. Living institutions of Rome and their followers, *"the third part of trees...and all green grass,"* burnt up because of the fire of new commitment.

And the second angel sounded, and as it were a great mountain burning with fire was cast into the sea: and the third part of the sea became blood; And the third part of the creatures which were in the sea, and had life, died; and the third part of the ships were destroyed. (8-9)

The second trumpet sounded when Christianity was as a mountain burning with fire of the Spirit for it carried the light of God. Its teachings, cast into the sea of Roman belief, competed with mystery cults and ancient religions. In periods of Christian persecution there was loss of physical and spiritual life (apostasy). Concerted effort was made to stamp out Christianity and to destroy its churches (Ships). Suffering of Christians became dreadful because of persecutions initiated by Diocletian and terminated by Galerius in 311 AD. In 313 Maximin urged toleration.[38] "Early in 313 Constantine met Licinus at Milan, and they agreed upon the terms of a letter concerning the Christians..."[39]

And the third angel sounded, and there fell a great star from heaven, burning as it were a lamp, and it fell upon the third part of the rivers, and upon the fountains of waters; And the name of the star is called Wormwood: and the third part of the waters became wormwood; and many men died of the waters, because they were made bitter. And the fourth angel sounded, and the third part of the sun was smitten, and the third part of the moon, and the third part of the stars; so as the third part of them was darkened, and the day shone not for a third part of it, and the night likewise. (10-12)

The blast of the third trumpet sounded and a star fell from heaven. Religious leaders sometime deviate from the covenant of God, and then a star from heaven falls. Various stars fell in the struggle to define Christian Creed. Constantine, with the dim light of a lamp, sought definitive spiritual understanding in hopes of creating unity and of preserving the empire. Councils in the Greek world established doctrine of Christology. By 381 AD the Nicene Creed was firmed. Division and separation within the Christian community caused some spiritual waters to become bitter as with the controversy of Arius.

By the fourth century, Christianity became the state religion, and the fourth trumpet encountered a church that had become intolerant to pagan and some forms of Christian teachings. Public worship, other than Christianity, was illegal in the Roman Empire by the end of the century. The church had moved from persecuted to persecutor, and the sun, moon and stars of early spiritual teachings were darkened.

Religious controversies and distinctions which when combined with differences of culture and government, led to growing separation of Eastern Orthodox from Western Roman Christianity. This difficulty, coupled with barbaric attacks and the fall of the Western Empire in 476 AD, led to the dark ages when a third part of the Christian Day, or Dispensation, was in

---

[38] Robert M. Grant, *Augustus to Constantine*, Harper and Row, p. 233.
[39] Ibid, p. 236

darkness. For several centuries there were schisms and heresies. By 1054 AD the East-West division of Christianity was complete.

From earlier times, some Christian churches with variation in thinking about the nature of Christ formed in Egypt and the Middle East. Some were Nestorian and some were Monophysite. Four national districts included Egyptian Coptic, Syrian Jacobite, Abyssinian, and Armenian.[40]

Angel Announces Three Woes to Come

And I beheld, and heard an angel flying through the midst of heaven, saying with a loud voice, Woe, woe, woe, to the inhabiters of the earth by reason of the other voices of the trumpet of the three angels, which are yet to sound! (13)

An angel flying through the midst of heaven announces the coming of three religious renewals beyond Christian predominance (in Western Civilization) and their accompanying periods of woe, which will be announced by the trumpet blasts of three future angels.

> Among the bounties of God is revelation. Hence revelation is progressive and continuous. It never ceases. It is necessary that the reality of Divinity with all its perfections and attributes should become resplendent in the human world. The reality of Divinity is like an endless ocean. Revelation may be likened to the rain.[41]

Each new revelation from God comes at a time that can be characterized as a condition of social woe. These three revelations, anticipated by the Book of Revelation and announced by way of the remaining trumpets voices, will ultimately lead to the goal of creating a spiritual humanity and a global society. But, even so, additional revelations will occur as required for maintenance of the future well being of humanity.

---

[40] Thomas P Neill, Ph. D., Raymond H Schmandt, Ph. D., *History of the Catholic Church*, The Bruce Publishing Co., p.97.
[41] 'Abdu'l-Bahá, *Promulgation of Universal Peace*, Bahá'í Publishing Trust, Wilmette, Illinois, p. 373.

Revelation Chapter 9

Fifth Angel Sounds Bottomless Pit

And the fifth angel sounded, and I saw a star fall from heaven unto the earth: and to him was given the key of the bottomless pit. And he opened the bottomless pit; and there arose a smoke out of the pit, as the smoke of a great furnace; and the sun and the air were darkened by reason of the smoke of the pit. (1-2)

A star fell from heaven when the fifth trumpet sounded, and *"he opened"* the bottomless pit of error.[42] He is a star or leader of Islam. Abu-Sufian, the son of Harb, was the leading man of the House of Umayyah; he and his son, Mu'áwíyah, succeeded in gaining control of Islam about three decades after the death of Muhammad. They held secular and political ambitions and from the beginning had been zealous enemies of Muhammad. They and the Umayyads, generally, were cause for grave difficulties; they blocked the power of the sun of truth and the encompassing air of sustenance.

Usurpation of Islamic administrative authority by the Umayyads is a running theme in the Book of Revelation as disclosed in Chapters 11-13. The characteristics of the pit develop into a paradigm of disunity and other related difficulties. Abu Sufian and Mu'áwíyah by virtue of their leadership role were *"stars"* of Islam and caused internal dissension to rise because of their embracing characteristics from out of the bottomless pit of error.

Islamic Warriors

And there came out of the smoke locusts upon the earth: and unto them was given power, as the scorpions of the earth have power. And it was commanded them that they should not hurt the grass of the earth, neither any green thing, neither any tree; but only those men which have not the seal of God in their foreheads. (3-4)

---

[42] 'Abdu'l-Bahá, *Some Answered Questions,* Bahá'í Publishing Trust, Wilmette, Illinois, p. 51.

Appearing from the smoke of conflict, Islamic warriors (locusts) had power of conquest but were ordered by Islamic writings not to hurt living things. Grass, green things and trees signify organic life forms that can be compared to people and their living institutions, p. 81. The warrior locusts were allowed to hurt only those men who did not have in their forehead the seal of God, which can be seen as recognizable spiritual and religious qualities. They were to hurt not the people of the Book—Jews, and Christians.

And to them it was given that they should not kill them, but that they should be tormented five months: and their torment was as the torment of a scorpion, when he striketh a man. And in those days shall men seek death, and shall not find it; and shall desire to die, and death shall flee from them. (5-6)

Islam conquered its vast territories reaching from Spain to India within a prophetic period of five months. By prophecy, five months is equal to one hundred fifty days or the same number of years, see Appendix. For a period of 150 years of conquest and consolidation, the locusts could torment the people of the Book, but the Arabian warriors were not to physically kill the Jews and Christians. Conquered peoples received Muhammad's spiritual message from Islamic warriors; there was no avoidance of His Teachings.

Under the Umayyads, Muslims captured the Maghreb (North Africa), Spain, and Portugal, marched across Europe until they were halted in the heart of France by Charles Martel at the Battle of Tours in 732, and extended the empire's borders to the Indian subcontinent.[43]

And the shapes of the locusts were like unto horses prepared unto battle; and on their heads were as it were crowns like gold, and their faces were as the faces of men. And they had hair as the hair of women, and their teeth were as the teeth of lions. And they had breastplates, as it were breastplates of iron; and the sound of their wings was as the sound of chariots of many horses running to battle. And they had tails like unto scorpions, and there were stings in their tails: and their power was to hurt men five months. (7-10)

---

[43] John L. Esposito, *Islam, The Straight Path,* Oxford University Press, p. 42.

Early Islamic warriors wore *"crowns like gold,"* the symbol of significant spiritual authority, and conquered in the name of religion. Warriors were able to hurt men for five months or one hundred fifty years, but the Umayyads lost their political power to the 'Abbásids in 750 AD.[44]

> The early centuries of 'Abbásid rule were marked by an unparalleled splendor and economic prosperity whose magnificence came to be immortalized in the Arabian Nights (The Thousand and One Nights), with its legendary exploits of the exemplary caliph, Harun al-Rashid (reigned 786-809). In a departure from the past, 'Abbásid success was based not on conquest, but on trade, commerce, industry, and agriculture.[45]

Therefore it was a little less than 150 years from Umayyad take over in 661 AD, and continuation of conquests, to the early flowering of Islam under the administration of the 'Abbásids.

And they had a king over them, which is the angel of the bottomless pit, whose name in the Hebrew tongue is Abaddon, but in the Greek tongue hath his name Apollyon. One woe is past; and, behold, there come two woes more hereafter. (11-12)

Within the Umayyad family and its controlling dynasty, initiated by their Chief, Abu-Sufian, usurpation of Muslim authority was assumed by 15 leaders, having, without repetition, 10 distinct names. Operating from the pit of error and placing emphasis on secular qualities, their king was a destroyer[46] of spiritual qualities. Abu-Sufian, as instigator, qualifies as the angel and king of the *"bottomless pit."*[47]

The Faith of Islam marks: *"One woe is past ... [but] there come two woes more hereafter."*

From this short discussion of Islam, twelve-verses, reference to one woe being past must be considered in the context of a general introduction

---

[44] Ibid, p. 52.
[45] Ibid, p. 53.
[46] 'Abdu'l-Bahá, *Some Answered Questions,* Bahá'í Publishing Trust, Wilmette, Illinois, p. 51.
[47] Ibid, p. 70.

along with the specific introduction of the bottomless pit. The initial look at Islam is over, but the importance of the Islamic Faith to the Book of Revelation continues to unfold in remaining chapters.

Sixth Angel Loosens Restraints

And the sixth angel sounded, and I heard a voice from the four horns of the golden altar which is before God, Saying to the sixth angel which had the trumpet, Loose the four angels which are bound in the great river Euphrates. And the four angels were loosed, which were prepared for an hour, and a day, and a month, and a year, for to slay the third part of men. (13-15)

John heard a voice of authority from the golden altar before God. The Father advises the sixth angel with trumpet to initiate the winds of change that were held until the servants could be sealed, vv 7:1-3, p. 81. The trumpet blast calls attention to a connection between the end of Eastern Orthodox Christianity and the end of Islam, its period of woe, and the beginning of the Bábí Faith. Further declaration of the second woe and its associated religion, the Bábí Faith, is made in Chapter 11.

Four angels bound to the region of the Euphrates[48]—Jewish, Christian, Muslim and Zoroastrian—represent religions previous to the Bábí and Bahá'í time periods that become freed for nearly the next four centuries, as follows:

"Four angels were loosed, which were prepared for an hour, and a day, and a month, and a year, for to slay the third part of men." The prophetic time span is 391 years: day equals year, month equals thirty days or years, and a year equals three hundred sixty days or years. (See Appendix) These add to 391 years. This time period spans from the conquest of Constantinople in 1453 AD, by the Ottoman Empire under the banner of Islam, to the birth of the Bábí revelation in 1844 AD.[49] The earlier date also marks the end of the Roman Empire, which was the champion of Eastern Orthodox Christianity. And the latter date marks the end of the Islamic Dispensation.

The religions and warriors from among their respective countries had attempted over the centuries the conquest of Constantinople. Now, with

---

[48] Hushidar Motlagh, *I Shall Come Again,* Global Perspective, Mt. Pleasant, Michigan, p. 305.
[49] Ibid, p. 306.

conquest of Constantinople and shifting of power to the east, these religions were free until the Hand of God would once more bring new revelation. Though Constantinople was a stronghold of Eastern Orthodox Christianity, Roman Catholics had previously sacked this city during the Fourth Crusade. Religious animosities remain even to the ethnic Balkan wars of 1999.

And the number of the army of the horsemen was two hundred thousand thousand: and I heard the number of them. And thus I saw the horses in the vision, and them that sat on them, having breastplates of fire, and of jacinth, and brimstone: and the heads of the horses were as the heads of lions; and out of their mouths issued fire and smoke and brimstone. By these three was the third part of men killed, by the fire, and by the smoke, and by the brimstone, which issued out of their mouths. For their power is in their mouth, and in their tails: for their tails were like unto serpents, and had heads, and with them they do hurt. (16-19)

The difficulties of this period, centering on the conquest of Constantinople, resulted in greater separation of western and eastern Christianity, and represents the loss (to cut-off or slay) of one third of Christianity, or all of Eastern Orthodox Christianity. As indicated above, the prophesied time span of 391 years connects the fall of Eastern Orthodox Christianity with the end of the Islamic Dispensation and the birth of its offspring the Bábí Faith that is accompanied by the second period of woe.

Islamic Conquest of the fortified city of Constantinople, under the Ottomans, was a difficult military task that used advanced weapons of that time. Cannons hurled 1200-pound projectiles.[50]

And the rest of the men which were not killed by these plagues yet repented not of the works of their hands, that they should not worship devils, and idols of gold, and silver, and brass, and stone, and of wood: which neither can see, nor hear, nor walk: Neither repented they of their murders, nor of their sorceries, nor of their fornication, nor of their thefts. (20-21)

---

[50] Robert F Riggs, *The Apocalypse Revealed*, Philosophical Library, New York, p. 140.

"And the rest of the men … repented … [not—of their] murders, nor of their sorceries, nor of their fornication, nor of their thefts." The evolution of God's Cause has had many difficulties that have led to the present segmented conditions of the Western and the Eastern Worlds.

Little Book
Chapter 10

The Law of God is divided into two parts. One is the fundamental basis which comprises all spiritual things ... it is faith, knowledge, certitude, justice, piety, righteousness, trustworthiness, love of God, benevolence, purity, detachment, humility, meekness, patience and constancy ... These virtues of humanity will be renewed in each of the different cycles [of religion]; for at the end of every cycle the spiritual Law of God - that is to say, the human virtues - disappears, and only the form subsists ... These foundations of the Religion of God, which are spiritual and which are the virtues of humanity, cannot be abrogated ... they are irremovable and eternal, and are renewed in the cycle of every Prophet. ... The second part of the Religion of God, which refers to the material world, and which comprises fasting, prayer, forms of worship, marriage and divorce, the abolition of slavery, legal processes, transactions, indemnities for murder, violence, theft and injuries - this part of the Law of God, which refers to material things, is modified and altered in each prophetic cycle in accordance with the necessities of the times.

Some Answered Questions, pp. 47-48

Revelation Chapter 10

A Little Book is Opened

And I saw another mighty angel come down from heaven, clothed with a cloud: and a rainbow was upon his head, and his face was as it were the sun, and his feet as pillars of fire: And he had in his hand a little book open: and he set his right foot upon the sea, and his left foot on the earth, And cried with a loud voice, as when a lion roareth: and when he had cried, seven thunders uttered their voices. (1-3)

Commenting on the holy Prophets, Bahá'u'lláh stated:

> At another time, Thou didst adorn Him with the name of Him Who was Thy Spirit (Jesus), and didst send Him down out of the heaven of Thy will, for the edification of Thy people, infusing thereby the spirit of life into the hearts of the sincere among Thy servants and the faithful among Thy creatures.[51]

John sees still another episode of renewal from a mighty angel, portraying a Prophet, who has spiritual radiance as bright as the sun and standing on pillars of love for God (fire of the Word). He brings the book of God, inherently small; that man has enlarged by voluminous additions of traditions and theology.

> The door of the knowledge of the Ancient of Days being thus closed in the face of all beings, the Source of infinite grace, according to His saying, "His grace hath transcended all things; My grace hath encompassed them all," hath caused those luminous Gems of Holiness to appear out of the realm of the spirit, in the noble form of the human temple, and be made manifest unto all men, that they may impart unto the world the mysteries of the

---

[51] Bahá'u'lláh, *Prayers and Meditations,* Bahá'í Publishing Trust, Wilmette, Illinois, p. 50

unchangeable Being, and tell of the subtleties of His imperishable Essence.[52]

This symbolic spiritual appearance represents the return of Jesus. Fulfilled by the Báb, His description is reminiscent of the Father, vv. 1:12-16. The reality of the Báb, as with the Father, comes from the world of spiritual truth—the home of the Prophet and source of revelation—and is clothed with clouds of obscurity. In the station of precursor to Bahá'u'lláh, He carries upon His head the covenant of God (rainbow).

> The Lord of the universe hath never raised up a prophet nor hath He sent down a Book unless He hath established His covenant with all men, calling for their acceptance of the next Revelation and of the next Book; inasmuch as the outpourings of His bounty are ceaseless and without limit.[53]

The Prophet is the keeper of the Covenant because He participates in a succession of Voices, eternal in the past and eternal in the future, the recurring Spirit of God.

> The Prophets 'regarded as one and the same person' include the lesser Prophets as well, and not merely those who bring a 'Book.' The station is different, but They are Prophets and Their nature thus different from that of ours.[54]

The Báb brings His own "Book," the Bayan; nevertheless, He is the precursor to Bahá'u'lláh. In stance, He spans a gap with right foot on the sea of spiritual sources and left foot on the firm ground of belief. This is the posture of the Prophet who draws spiritual attention with cry as powerful as that of a lion. Response, with the sound of thunder, is heard from seven past Prophets—the seven Spirits of God.

---

[52] Bahá'u'lláh, *Gleanings from the Writings of Bahá'u'lláh,* Bahá'í Publishing Trust, Wilmette, Illinois, p. 47

[53] Báb, *Selections from the Writings of the Báb,* Bahá'í World Centre, Haifa p. 87.

[54] Gertrude Garrida, *Directives From The Guardian*, Bahá'í Publishing Trust, New Delhi, p. 58.

Seal the Voice of the Thunders

And when the seven thunders had uttered their voices, I was about to write: and I heard a voice from heaven saying unto me, Seal up those things which the seven thunders uttered, and write them not. (4)

John was informed that the time was not appropriate for disclosure about the way to the future; he should *"seal up"* or not make known the seven thunders' message, which carries thoughts or confessions of the seven Spirits of God.

Last Trumpet to Remove the Mystery

And the angel which I saw stand upon the sea and upon the earth lifted up his hand to heaven, And sware by him that liveth for ever and ever, who created heaven, and the things that therein are, and the earth, and the things that therein are, and the sea, and the things which are therein, that there should be time no longer: But in the days of the voice of the seventh angel, when he shall begin to sound, the mystery of God should be finished, as he hath declared to his servants the prophets. (5-7)

The angel with the book makes an important statement about timing. He swore to God, who has created all things, that in the days of the voice of the seventh angel there should be time no longer. The mystery of God shall be over when the period of the third woe is introduced by the seventh trumpet—then the way to the future is explainable.

The Báb and His religion, the Bábí Faith, carried forth the precursor function of the religious process. His situation is similar to John the Baptist in relation to Jesus Christ, but with a difference: He not only brought revelation and religious renewal but closed the Cycle of Prophecy.

John Studies The Little Book

And the voice which I heard from heaven spake unto me again, and said, Go and take the little book which is open in the hand of the angel which standeth upon the sea and upon the earth. And I went unto the angel, and said unto him, Give me the little book. And he said unto me, Take it, and eat it up; and it shall make thy belly bitter, but it shall be in thy mouth sweet as honey. (8-9)

John was instructed on the little book: *"Take it, and eat it up;"* that is, read and understand. Its teachings are emotionally tasteful, *"sweet as honey,"* but its laws can be difficult to apply and *"make thy belly bitter."* An example is seen in the need for elimination of all forms of prejudice in a society of diverse cultures.

The Law of God, as renewed, is sometimes in conflict with existing social habits and then becomes a barrier for many to accepting God's new requirements. But indirect aid to God's Cause might occur. This can happen when disturbances, unbeknown to the perpetrators, create individual and institutional responses that indirectly support movement toward a global civilization. This is seen in respect to the world wars, the cold war, and ethnic wars, all of which have been fought because of political, economic and religious power struggles. These battles all demonstrate the need for a global society, which supports an international military force and a United Nations type organization. Worldwide policing is too much of a burden for any one country by itself.

Thou Must Prophesy

And I took the little book out of the angel's hand, and ate it up; and it was in my mouth sweet as honey: and as soon as I had eaten it, my belly was bitter. And he said unto me, Thou must prophesy again before many peoples, and nations, and tongues, and kings. (10-11)

John took the little book and *"ate it up"* by studying its meaning. John is a servant, and servants must take the message before many peoples, nations, tongues, and kings; they make known the teachings of new revelation. The Law of God, as contained in the little book, is required to combat, among others, the administrative distortions caused by the influence of the pit of error, opened in verse 9:1.

Revelation from God brings spiritual renewal and supports social advancement. God's message, in this age, is universal and brings teachings for the purpose of *world unity* and *world peace.*

Islam

Chapters 11-13

The major social achievement of Muhammad's ministry was the welding together of a hundred or more disparate and feuding tribes into one nation ... So powerful was the impetus given to this nation by Islam that within one generation it had conquered territory stretching from Tunisia to the borders of India and within a few generations this backward and primitive people became the center of civilization in the Western world and remained thus for almost four hundred years.

Shi'i Islam, p. 9

Revelation Chapter 11

The Law of God

And there was given me a reed like unto a rod: and the angel stood, saying, Rise, and measure the temple of God, and the altar, and them that worship therein. But the court which is without the temple leave out, and measure it not; for it is given unto the Gentiles: and the holy city shall they tread under foot forty and two months. (1-2)

This reed is a Perfect Man Who is likened to a reed, and the manner of its likeness is this: when the interior of a reed is empty and free from all matter, it will produce beautiful melodies; and as the sound and melodies do not come from the reed, but from the flute player who blows upon it, so the sanctified heart of that blessed Being is free and emptied from all save God, pure and exempt from the attachments of all human conditions, and is the companion of the Divine Spirit. Whatever He utters is not from Himself, but from the real flute player, and it is a divine inspiration. That is why He is likened to a reed; and that reed is like a rod - that is to say, it is the helper of every impotent one, and the support of human beings. It is the rod of the Divine Shepherd by which He guards His flock and leads them about the pastures of the Kingdom. (Presented commentary for this Chapter is from 'Abdu'l-Bahá.[55])

'The angel stood, saying, Rise, and measure the temple of God, and the altar, and them that worship therein' - that is to say, compare and measure: measuring is the discovery of proportion. Thus the angel said: compare the temple of God and the altar and them that are praying therein - that is to say, investigate what is their true condition and discover in what degree and state they are, and what conditions, perfections, behavior and attributes they possess; and make

---

[55] 'Abdu'l-Bahá, *Some Answered Questions,* Bahá'í Publishing Trust, Wilmette, Illinois, Chapter 11.

yourself cognizant of the mysteries of those holy souls who dwell in the Holy of Holies in purity and sanctity.

'But the court which is without the temple leave out, and measure it not; for it is given unto the Gentiles.' In the beginning of the seventh century after Christ, when Jerusalem was conquered, the Holy of Holies was outwardly preserved - that is to say, the house, which Solomon built; but outside the Holy of Holies the outer court was taken and given to the Gentiles.

'And the holy city shall they tread under foot forty and two months' - that is to say, the Gentiles shall govern and control Jerusalem forty and two months, signifying twelve hundred and sixty days; and as each day signifies a year, by this reckoning it becomes twelve hundred and sixty years, which is the duration of the cycle of the Qur'an. For in the texts of the Holy Book, each day is a year; as it is said in the fourth chapter of Ezekiel, verse 6: 'Thou shalt bear the iniquity of the house of Judah forty days: I have appointed thee each day for a year.'

This prophesies the duration of the Dispensation of Islam when Jerusalem was trodden under foot, which means that it lost its glory - but the Holy of Holies was preserved, guarded and respected - until the year 1260. This twelve hundred and sixty years is a prophecy of the manifestation of the Báb, the 'Gate' of Bahá'u'lláh, which took place in the year 1260 of the Hejira [beginning of the Islamic calendar] of Muhammad, and as the period of twelve hundred and sixty years has expired, Jerusalem, the Holy City, is now beginning to become prosperous, populous and flourishing. Anyone who saw Jerusalem sixty years ago, and who sees it now, will recognize how populous and flourishing it has become, and how it is again honored.

This is the outward meaning of these verses of the Revelation of St. John; but they have another explanation and a symbolic sense, which is as follows: the Law of God is divided into two parts.

One is the fundamental basis which comprises all spiritual things - that is to say, it refers to the spiritual virtues and divine qualities; this does not change nor alter: it is the Holy of Holies, which is the essence of the Law of Adam, Noah, Abraham, Moses, Christ, Muhammad, the Báb, and Bahá'u'lláh, and which lasts and is established in all the prophetic cycles. It will never be abrogated, for it is spiritual and not material truth; it is faith, knowledge, certitude, justice, piety, righteousness, trustworthiness, love of God, benevolence, purity, detachment, humility, meekness, patience and constancy. It shows mercy to the poor, defends the oppressed, gives to the wretched and uplifts the fallen.

These divine qualities, these eternal commandments, will never be abolished; nay, they will last and remain established forever and ever. These virtues of humanity will be renewed in each of the different cycles; for at the end of every cycle the spiritual Law of God - that is to say, the human virtues - disappears, and only the form subsists.

Thus among the Jews, at the end of the cycle of Moses, which coincides with the Christian manifestation, the Law of God disappeared, only a form without spirit remaining. The Holy of Holies departed from among them, but the outer court of Jerusalem - which is the expression used for the form of the religion - fell into the hands of the Gentiles. In the same way, the fundamental principles of the religion of Christ, which are the greatest virtues of humanity, have disappeared; and its form has remained in the hands of the clergy and the priests. Likewise, the foundation of the religion of Muhammad has disappeared, but its form remains in the hands of the official ulama. These foundations of the Religion of God, which are spiritual and which are the virtues of humanity, cannot be abrogated; they are irremovable and eternal, and are renewed in the cycle of every Prophet.

The second part of the Religion of God, which refers to the material world, and which comprises fasting, prayer, forms of wor-

ship, marriage and divorce, the abolition of slavery, legal processes, transactions, indemnities for murder, violence, theft and injuries - this part of the Law of God, which refers to material
things, is modified and altered in each prophetic cycle in accordance with the necessities of the times.

Briefly, what is meant by the term Holy of Holies is that spiritual
Law which will never be modified, altered or abrogated; and the
Holy City means the material Law, which may be abrogated; and
this material Law, which is described as the Holy City, was to be
trodden under foot for twelve hundred and sixty years.

Prophet as Lord

*And I will give power unto my two witnesses, and they shall prophesy a thousand two
hundred and three-score days, clothed in sackcloth. (3)*

These two witnesses are Muhammad the Messenger of God, and
Alí, son of Abu Talib.

In the Qur'an it is said that God addressed Muhammad, the Messenger of God, saying: *'We made You a Witness, a Herald of good
news, and a Warner.'** - that is to say, We have established Thee as
the witness, the giver of good tidings, and as One bringing the
wrath of God. The meaning of *'a witness'* is one by whose testimony things may be verified. The commands of these two witnesses were to be performed for twelve hundred and sixty days,
each day signifying a year. Now, Muhammad was the root, and
Alí the branch, like Moses and Joshua. It is said they 'are clothed
in sackcloth,' meaning that they, apparently, were to be clothed in
old raiment, not in new raiment; in other words, in the beginning
they would possess no splendor in the eyes of the people, nor
would their Cause appear new; for Muhammad's spiritual Law
corresponds to that of Christ in the Gospel, and most of His laws
relating to material things correspond to those of the Pentateuch.
This is the meaning of the old raiment.

*Persian translation of the Arabic Text of the Qur'an.

These are the two olive trees, and the two candlesticks standing before the God of the earth. (4)

These two souls are likened to olive trees because at that time all lamps were lighted by olive oil. The meaning is two persons from whom that spirit of the wisdom of God, which is the cause of the illumination of the world, appears. These lights of God were to radiate and shine; therefore, they are likened to two candlesticks: the candlestick is the abode of the light, and from it the light shines forth. In the same way the light of guidance would shine and radiate from these illumined souls.

'They are standing before God,' meaning that they are standing in the service of God, and educating the creatures of God, such as the barbarous nomad Arab tribes of the Arabian Peninsula, whom they educated in such a way that in those days they reached the highest degree of civilization, and their fame and renown became worldwide.

And if any man would hurt them, fire proceedeth out of their mouth, and devoureth their enemies…(5)

That is to say, that no one would be able to withstand them, that if a person wished to belittle their teachings and their law, he would be surrounded and exterminated by this same law which proceedeth out of their mouth; and everyone who attempted to injure, to antagonize and to hate them would be destroyed by a command which would come out of their mouth. And thus it happened: all their enemies were vanquished, put to flight and annihilated. In this most evident way God assisted them.

These have power to shut heaven, that it rain not in the days of their prophecy, They have power over water to turn it to blood, (6)

'These have power to shut heaven, that it rain not in the days of their prophecy,' meaning that in that cycle they would be like kings. The law and teachings of Muhammad, and the explanations and commentaries of Alí, are a heavenly bounty; if they wish to give this bounty, they have power to do so. If they do not wish it, the rain will not fall: in this connection rain stands for bounty.

'They have power over water to turn it to blood,' meaning that the prophet -hood of Muhammad was the same as that of Moses, and that the power of Alí was the same as that of Joshua: if they wished, they could turn the water of the Nile into blood, so far as the Egyptians and those who denied them were concerned - that is to say, that that which was the cause of their life, through their ignorance and pride, became the cause of their death. So the kingdom, wealth and power of Pharaoh and his people, which were the causes of the life of the nation, became, through their opposition, denial and pride, the cause of death, destruction, dispersion, degradation and poverty. Hence these two witnesses have power to destroy the nations.

'And smite the earth with all plagues, as often as they will,' meaning that they also would have the power and the material force necessary to educate the wicked and those who are oppressors and tyrants, for to these two witnesses God granted both outward and inward power, that they might educate and correct the ferocious, bloodthirsty, tyrannical nomad Arabs, who were like beasts of prey.

Martyrdom of the Prophet

And when they shall have finished their testimony, The beast that ascendeth out of the bottomless pit shall war against them, and shall overcome them, and kill them: (7)

'And when they shall have finished their testimony,' means when they should have performed that which they are commanded, and should have delivered the divine message, promoting the Law of God and propagating the heavenly teachings, to the intent that the signs of spiritual life might be manifest in souls, and the light of the virtues of the world of humanity might shine forth, until

complete development should be brought about among the no-mad tribes.

'The beast that ascendeth out of the bottomless pit shall war against them, and shall overcome them, and kill them:' - this beast means the Umay-yads who attacked them from the pit of error, and who rose against the religion of Muhammad and against the reality of Alí - in other words, the love of God.

'The beast made war against these two witnesses' - that is to say, a spiri-tual war, meaning that the beast would act in entire opposition to the teachings, customs and institutions of these two witnesses, to such an extent that the virtues and perfections which were dif-fused by the power of those two witnesses among the peoples and tribes would be entirely dispelled, and the animal nature and carnal desires would conquer. Therefore, this beast making war against them would gain the victory - meaning that the darkness of error coming from this beast was to have ascendancy over the horizons of the world, and kill those two witnesses - in other words, that it would destroy the spiritual life which they spread abroad in the midst of the nation, and entirely remove the divine laws and teachings, treading under foot the Religion of God. Nothing would thereafter remain but a lifeless body without spirit.

And their dead bodies shall lie in the street of the great city, which spiritually is called Sodom and Egypt, where also our Lord was crucified. (8)

'Their bodies' means the Religion of God, and *'the street'* means in public view. The meaning of *'Sodom and Egypt,'* the place *'where also our Lord was crucified,'* is this region of Syria, and especially Jerusa-lem, where the Umayyads then had their dominions; and it was here that the Religion of God and the divine teachings first dis-appeared, and a body without spirit remained. *'Their bodies'* repre-sents the Religion of God, which remained like a dead body without spirit.

111

And they of the people and kindreds and tongues and nations shall see their dead bodies three days and a half, and shall not suffer their dead bodies to be put in graves. (9)

As it was before explained, in the terminology of the Holy Books three days and a half signify three years and a half, and three years and a half are forty and two months, and forty and two months twelve hundred and sixty days; and as each day by the text of the Holy Book signifies one year, the meaning is that for twelve hundred and sixty years, which is the cycle of the Qur'an, the nations, tribes and peoples would look at their bodies - that is to say, that they would make a spectacle of the Religion of God: though they would not act in accordance with it, still, they would not suffer their bodies - meaning the Religion of God - to be put in the grave. That is to say, that in appearance they would cling to the Religion of God and not allow it to completely disappear from their midst, nor the body of it to be entirely destroyed and annihilated. Nay, in reality they would leave it, while outwardly preserving its name and remembrance.

Those *'kindreds, people and nations'* signify those who are gathered under the shadow of the Qur'an, not permitting the Cause and Law of God to be, in outward appearance, entirely destroyed and annihilated - for there are prayer and fasting among them - but the fundamental principles of the Religion of God, which are morals and conduct, with the knowledge of divine mysteries, have disappeared; the light of the virtues of the world of humanity, which is the result of the love and knowledge of God, is extinguished; and the darkness of tyranny, oppression, satanic passions and desires has become victorious. The body of the Law of God, like a corpse, has been exposed to public view for twelve hundred and sixty days, each day being counted as a year, and this period is the cycle of Muhammad.

The people forfeited all that these two persons had established, which was the foundation of the Law of God, and destroyed the virtues of the world of humanity, which are the divine gifts and the spirit of this religion, to such a degree that truthfulness, justice, love, union, purity, sanctity, detachment and all the divine qualities departed from among them. In the religion only prayers and fasting persisted; this condition lasted for twelve hundred and sixty years, which is the duration of the cycle of the Furqan.* It was as if these two persons were dead, and their bodies were remaining without spirit.

*Another name for the Qur'an, signifying the distinction.

And they that dwell upon the earth shall rejoice over them, and make merry, and shall send gifts to one another, because these two prophets tormented them that dwelt on the earth. (10)

'*Those who dwelt upon the earth*' means the other nations and races, such as the peoples of Europe and distant Asia, who, when they saw that the character of Islam was entirely changed, the Law of God forsaken—that virtues, zeal and honor had departed from among them, and that their qualities were changed—became happy, and rejoiced that corruption of morals had infected the people of Islam, and that they would in consequence be overcome by other nations. So this thing has come to pass. Witness this people, which had attained the summit of power, how degraded and downtrodden it is now.

The other nations '*shall send gifts to one another,*' meaning that they should help each other, for '*these two prophets tormented them that dwelt upon the earth*' -that is, they overcame the other nations and peoples of the world and conquered them.

Resurrection of the Prophet

And after three days and a half the spirit of life from God entered into them, and they stood upon their feet; and great fear fell upon them that saw them. (11)

Three days and a half, as we before explained, is twelve hundred and sixty years. Those two persons whose bodies were lying spiritless are the teachings and the law that Muhammad established and Alí promoted, from which, however, the reality had departed and only the form remained. The spirit came again into them means that those foundations and teachings were again established. In other words, the spirituality of the Religion of God had been changed into materiality, and virtues into vices; the love of God had been changed into hatred, enlightenment into darkness, divine qualities into satanic ones, justice into tyranny, mercy into enmity, sincerity into hypocrisy, guidance into error, and purity into sensuality. Then after three days and a half, which by the terminology of the Holy Books is twelve hundred and sixty years, these divine teachings, heavenly virtues, perfections and spiritual bounties were again renewed by the appearance of the Báb and the devotion of Jinab-i-Quddus.*

The holy breezes were diffused, the light of truth shone forth, the season of the life-giving spring came, and the morn of guidance dawned. These two lifeless bodies again became living, and these two great ones - one the Founder and the other the promoter - arose and were like two candlesticks, for they illumined the world with the light of truth.

*Hájí Mullá Muhammad-'Alíy-í-Bárfurúshí, one of the chief disciples of the Báb and one of the nineteen Letters of the Living.

And they heard a great voice from heaven saying unto them, Come up hither. And they ascended up to heaven, And their enemies beheld them, (12)

'*And they heard a great voice from heaven saying unto them, Come up hither. And they ascended up to heaven,*' meaning that from the invisible heaven they heard the voice of God, saying: You have performed all that was proper and fitting in delivering the teachings and glad tidings; you have given My message to the people and raised the call of God, and have accomplished your duty. Now, like Christ, you must sacrifice your life for the Well-Beloved, and be martyrs. And that Sun of Reality, and that Moon of Guid-

ance,* both, like Christ, set on the horizon of the greatest martyrdom and ascended to the Kingdom of God.

'*And their enemies beheld them,*' meaning that many of their enemies,
after witnessing their martyrdom, realized the sublimity of their
station and the exaltation of their virtue, and testified to their
greatness and perfection.

*The Báb and Jináb-i-Quddús

*And the same hour there was a great earthquake, and the tenth part of the city fell, and
in the earthquake were slain of men seven thousand. And the remnant was affrighted and
gave glory to the God of heaven. (13)*

This earthquake occurred in Shiraz after the martyrdom of the
Báb. The city was in a turmoil, and many people were destroyed.
Great agitation also took place through diseases, cholera, dearth,
scarcity, famine and afflictions, the like of which had never been
known.

'*And the remnant was affrighted and gave glory to the God of heaven.*'
When the earthquake took place in Fars, all the remnant lamented
and cried day and night, and were occupied in glorifying and
praying to God They were so troubled and affrighted that they
had no sleep nor rest at night.

The second woe is past; and, behold, the third woe cometh quickly. (14)

The first woe is the appearance of the Prophet, Muhammad, the
son of Abdu'llah - peace be upon Him! The second woe is that
of the Báb - to Him be glory and praise! The third woe is the
great day of the manifestation of the Lord of Hosts and the radiance of the Beauty of the Promised One. The explanation of this
subject, woe, is mentioned in the thirtieth chapter of Ezekiel,
where it is said: 'The word of the Lord came again unto me, say-

ing, Son of man, prophesy and say, Thus saith the Lord God;
Howl ye, Woe worth the day! For the day is near, even the day of
the Lord is near.' Ezek. 30:1-5.

Therefore, it is certain that the day of woe is the day of the Lord;
for in that day woe is for the neglectful, woe is for the sinners,
woe is for the ignorant. That is why it is said, 'The second woe is
past; behold the third woe cometh quickly.' This third woe is the
day of the manifestation of Bahá'u'lláh, the day of God; and it is
near to the day of the appearance of the Báb.

The Seventh Trumpet Sounded

*And the seventh angel sounded; and there were great voices in heaven, saying, The king-
doms of this world are become the kingdoms of our Lord, and of His Christ; and He
shall reign for ever and ever. (15)*

The seventh angel is a man qualified with heavenly attributes,
who will arise with heavenly qualities and character. Voices will
be raised, so that the appearance of the Divine Manifestation will
be proclaimed and diffused. In the day of the manifestation of
the Lord of Hosts, and at the epoch of the divine cycle of the
Omnipotent which is promised and mentioned in all the books
and writings of the Prophets - in that day of God, the Spiritual
and Divine Kingdom will be established, and the world will be
renewed; a new spirit will be breathed into the body of creation;
the season of the divine spring will come; the clouds of mercy
will rain; the sun of reality will shine; the life-giving breeze will
blow; the world of humanity will wear a new garment; the surface
of the earth will be a sublime paradise; mankind will be educated;
wars, disputes, quarrels and malignity will disappear; and truthfulness, righteousness, peace and the worship of God will appear;
union, love and brotherhood will surround the world; and God
will rule for evermore - meaning that the Spiritual and Everlasting
Kingdom will be established. Such is the day of God. For all the
days, which have come and gone were the days of Abraham,
Moses and Christ, or of the other Prophets; but this day is the

day of God, for the Sun of Reality will arise in it with the utmost warmth and splendor.

And the four and twenty elders, which sat before God on their seats, fell upon their faces, and worshipped God. Saying, We give Thee thanks, O Lord God Almighty, Which art, and wast, and art to come; because Thou hast taken to Thee Thy great power, and hast reigned. (16-17)

In each cycle the guardians and holy souls have been twelve. So Jacob had twelve sons; in the time of Moses there were twelve heads or chiefs of the tribes; in the time of Christ there were welve Apostles; and in the time of Muhammad there were twelve Imams. But in this glorious manifestation there are twenty-four, double the number of all the others, for the greatness of this manifestation requires it. These holy souls are in the presence of God seated on their own thrones, meaning that they reign eternally.

These twenty-four great persons, though they are seated on the thrones of everlasting rule, yet are worshipers of the appearance of the universal Manifestation, and they are humble and submissive, saying, *'We give thanks to Thee, O Lord God Almighty, Which art, and wast, and art to come, because Thou hast taken to Thee Thy great power and hast reigned'* - that is to say, Thou wilt issue all Thy teachings, Thou wilt gather all the people of the earth under Thy shadow, and Thou wilt bring all men under the shadow of one tent. Although it is the Eternal Kingdom of God, and He always had, and has, a Kingdom, the Kingdom here means the manifestation of Himself;* and He will issue all the laws and teachings which are the spirit of the world of humanity and everlasting life. And that universal Manifestation will subdue the world by spiritual power, not by war and combat; He will do it with peace and tranquillity, not by the sword and arms; He will establish this Heavenly Kingdom by true love, and not by the power of war. He will promote these divine teachings by kindness and righteousness, and not by weapons and harshness. He will so educate the nations and people that, notwithstanding their various conditions, their different customs and characters, and their diverse religions and races, they will, as it is said in the Bible, like the wolf and the lamb, the leopard, the kid, the sucking child and the serpent, become comrades, friends and companions. The contentions of races, the differences of religions, and the barriers between nations will be completely removed, and all will attain perfect union and reconciliation under the shadow of the Blessed Tree.

*i.e., His most complete manifestation.

And the nations were angry, and Thy wrath is come. And the time of the dead, that they should be judged. That Thou shouldst give reward unto Thy servants the prophets, and the saints, and them that fear Thy name, small and great. And shouldst destroy them which destroy the earth. (18)

'*And the nations were angry,*' for Thy teachings opposed the passions of the other peoples;

'*and Thy wrath is come.*' that is to say, all will be afflicted by evident loss; because they do not follow Thy precepts, counsels and teachings, they will be deprived of Thy everlasting bounty, and veiled from the light of the Sun of Reality.

'*And the time of the dead, that they should be judged.*' means that the time has come that the dead - that is to say, those who are deprived of the spirit of the love of God and have not a share of the sanctified eternal life - will be judged with justice, meaning they will arise to receive that which they deserve. He will make the reality of their secrets evident, showing what a low degree they occupy in the world of existence, and that in reality they are under the rule of death.

'That Thou shouldst give reward unto Thy servants the prophets, and the saints, and them that fear Thy name, small and great.' - that is to say, He will distinguish the righteous by endless bounty, making them shine on the horizon of eternal honor, like the stars of heaven. He will assist them by endowing them with behavior and actions, which are the light of the world of humanity, the cause of guidance, and the means of everlasting life in the Divine Kingdom.

'And shouldst destroy them which destroy the earth' means that He will entirely deprive the neglectful; for the blindness of the blind will be manifest, and the vision of the seers will be evident; the ignorance and want of knowledge of the people of error will be recognized, and the knowledge and wisdom of the people under guidance will be apparent; consequently, the destroyers will be destroyed.

And the temple of God was opened in heaven. And there was seen in His temple the ark of His Testament. And there were lightnings, and voices, and thunderings, and an earthquake, and great hail, (19)

'And the temple of God was opened in heaven.' means that the divine Jerusalem is found, and the Holy of Holies has become visible. The Holy of Holies, according to the terminology of the people of wisdom, is the essence of the Divine Law, and the heavenly and true teachings of the Lord, which have not been changed in the cycle of any Prophet, as it was before explained. The sanctuary of Jerusalem is likened to the reality of the Law of God, which is the Holy of Holies; and all the laws, conventions, rites and material regulations are the city of Jerusalem -this is why it is called the heavenly Jerusalem. Briefly, as in this cycle the Sun of Reality will make the light of God shine with the umost splendor, therefore, the essence of the teachings of God will be realized in the world of existence, and the darkness of ignorance and want of knowledge will be dispelled. The world will become a new world, and enlightenment will prevail. So the Holy of Holies will appear.

'*And the temple of God was opened in heaven*' means also that by the diffusion of the divine teachings, the appearance of these heavenly mysteries, and the rising of the Sun of Reality, the doors of success and prosperity will be opened in all directions, and the signs of goodness and heavenly benedictions will be made plain.

'*And there was seen in His temple the ark of His Testament.*' - that is to say, the Book of His Testament will appear in His Jerusalem, the Epistle of the Covenant will be established, and the meaning of the Testament and of the Covenant will bcome evident. The renown of God will overspread the East and West, and the proclamation of the Cause of God will fill the world. The violators of the Covenant will be degraded and dispersed, and the faithful cherished and glorified, for they cling to the Book of the Testament and are firm and steadfast in the Covenant.

'*And there were lightnings, and voices, and thunderings, and an earthquake, and great hail,*' meaning that after the appearance of the Book of the Testament there will be a great storm, and the lightnings of the anger and the wrath of God will flash, the noise of the thunder of the violation of the Covenant will resound, the earthquake of doubts will take place, the hail of torments will beat upon the violators of the Covenant, and even those who profess belief will fall into trials and temptations.

Revelation Chapter 12

Personifying the Law of God

And there appeared a great wonder in heaven; a woman clothed with the sun, and the moon under her feet, and upon her head a crown of twelve stars: (1)

This woman is that bride, the Law of God that descended upon Muhammad. The sun with which she was clothed, and the moon which was under her feet, are the two nations which are under the shadow of that Law, the Persian and Ottoman kingdoms; for the emblem of Persia is the sun, and that of the Ottoman Empire is the crescent moon. Thus the sun and moon are the emblems of two kingdoms, which are under the power of the Law of God. Afterward it is said: *"upon her head is a crown of twelve stars."* These twelve stars are the twelve Imams, who were the promoters of the Law of Muhammad and the educators of the people, shining like stars in the heaven of guidance. Then it is said in the second verse:[56]

and she being with child cried,... (2)

meaning that this Law fell into the greatest difficulties and endured great troubles and afflictions until a perfect offspring was produced - that is, the coming Manifestation, the Promised One, Who is the perfect offspring, and Who was reared in the bosom of this Law, which is as its mother. The child Who is referred to is the Báb, the Primal Point, Who was in truth born from the Law of Muhammad - that is to say, the Holy Reality, Who is the child and outcome of the Law of God, His mother, and Who is promised by that religion, finds a reality in the kingdom of that Law; but because of the despotism of the dragon the child was

---

[56] Ibid, Chapter 13, pp. 68-72.

carried up to God. After twelve hundred and sixty days the dragon was destroyed, and the child of the Law of God, the Promised One, became manifest.

The Dragon of Politics

And there appeared another wonder in heaven; and behold a great red dragon, having seven heads and ten horns, and seven crowns upon his heads. And his tail drew the third part of the stars of heaven, and did cast them to the earth... (3)

These signs are an allusion to the dynasty of the Umayyads who dominated the Mohammadan religion. Seven heads and seven crowns mean seven countries and dominions over which the Umayyads had power: they were the Roman dominion around Damascus; and the Persian, Arabian and Egyptian dominions, together with the dominion of Africa - that is to say, Tunis, Morocco and Algeria; the dominion of Andalusia, which is now Spain; and the dominion of the Turks of Transoxania. The Umayyads had power over these countries. The ten horns mean the names of the Umayyad rulers - that is, without repetition, there were ten names of rulers, meaning ten names of commanders and chiefs - the first is Abu Sufyan and the last Marvan - but several of them bear the same name. So there are two Muaviya, three Yazid, two Valid, and two Marvan; but if the names were counted without repetition there would be ten. The Umayyads, of whom the first was Abu Sufyan, Amir of Mecca and chief of the dynasty of the Umayyads, and the last was Marvan, destroyed the third part of the holy and saintly people of the lineage of Muhammad who were like the stars of heaven.

And the dragon stood before the woman which was ready to be delivered, for to devour the child as soon as it was born. (4)

As we have before explained, this woman is the Law of God. The dragon was standing near the woman to devour her child, and this child was the promised Manifestation, the offspring of the Law of Muhammad. The Umayyads were always waiting to get possession of the Promised One, Who was to come from the line of Muhammad, to destroy and annihilate Him; for they much feared the appearance of the promised Manifestation, and they sought to kill any of Muhammad's descendants who might be highly esteemed.

The Martyred Prophet

And she brought forth a man child, Who was to rule all nations with a rod of iron. And her child was caught up unto God, and to His throne. (5)

This great son is the promised Manifestation Who was born of the Law of God and reared in the bosom of the divine teachings. The iron rod is a symbol of power and might - it is not a sword - and means that with divine power and might He will shepherd all the nations of the earth. This son is the Báb.

'And her child was caught up unto God, and to His throne.' This is a prophecy of the Báb, Who ascended to the heavenly realm, to the Throne of God, and to the center of His Kingdom. Consider how all this corresponds to what happened.

And the woman fled into the wilderness. Where she had a place prepared of God. That they should feed her there a thousand two hundred and threescore days. (6)

'And the woman fled into the wilderness' - that is to say, the Law of God fled to the wilderness, meaning the vast desert of Hijaz, and the Arabian Peninsula.

'Where she had a place prepared of God.' The Arabian Peninsula became the abode and dwelling place, and the center of the Law of God.

'That they should feed her there a thousand two hundred and threescore days.' In the terminology of the Holy Book these twelve hundred and sixty days mean the twelve hundred and sixty years that the Law of God was set up in the wilderness of Arabia, the great desert:

from it the Promised One has come. After twelve hundred and sixty years that Law will have no more influence, for the fruit of that tree will have appeared, and the result will have been produced.

Consider how the prophecies correspond to one another. In the Apocalypse, the appearance of the Promised One is appointed after forty-two months, and Daniel expresses it as three times and a half, which is also forty-two months, which are twelve hundred and sixty days. In another passage of John's Revelation it is clearly spoken of as twelve hundred and sixty days, and in the Holy Book it is said that each day signifies one year. Nothing could be clearer than this agreement of the prophecies with one another. The Báb appeared in the year 1260 of the Hejira of Muhammad, which is the beginning of the universal era reckoning of all Islam. There are no clearer proofs than this in the Holy Books for any Manifestation. For him who is just, the agreement of the times indicated by the tongues of the Great Ones is the most conclusive proof. There is no other possible explanation of these prophecies. Blessed are the just souls who seek the truth. But failing justice, the people attack, dispute and openly deny the evidence, like the Pharisees who, at the manifestation of Christ, denied with the greatest obstinacy the explanations of Christ and of His disciples. They obscured Christ's Cause before the ignorant people, saying, *These prophecies are not of Jesus, but of the Promised One Who shall come later, according to the conditions mentioned in the Bible.'* Some of these conditions were that He must have a kingdom, be seated on the throne of David, enforce the Law of the Bible, and manifest such justice that the wolf and the lamb shall gather at the same spring.

And thus they prevented the people from knowing Christ.[57]

---

[57] Ibid.

War in Heaven

And there was war in heaven: Michael and his angels fought against the dragon; and the dragon fought and his angels, And prevailed not; neither was their place found any more in heaven. And the great dragon was cast out, that old serpent, called the Devil, and Satan, which deceiveth the whole world: he was cast out into the earth, and his angels were cast out with him. (7-9)

Following the seventh trumpet, Bahá'u'lláh and His followers proclaim the Word of God and thereby initiate a process of worldwide spiritual renewal. The new religion has traveled beyond its homeland and successfully encircled the globe. Although the *'great dragon...that old serpent, called the Devil, and Satan'* refers specifically, as a paradigm, to the affairs of the Umayyad Dynasty and the difficulties it has created, the whole world of this age suffers from many trials and discontinuities, and all humanity is in need of support and uplifting at this time.

And I heard a loud voice saying in heaven, Now is come salvation, and strength, and the kingdom of our God, and the power of his Christ: for the accuser of our brethren is cast down, which accused them before our God day and night. And they overcame him by the blood of the Lamb, and by the word of their testimony; and they loved not their lives unto the death. (10-11)

The battle with the beast, which has embraced deviations forthcoming from the bottomless pit of error, was fought spiritually in heaven when Michael (Bahá'u'lláh, revelator at the time of the third woe) and his angels cast out the dragon from within the *"kingdom of our God"* with *"power of his Christ."* God's Prophet in the station of the return of Jesus Christ is cause for renewal that was initiated by the Báb. After a short ministry of six years, *"and they loved not their lives unto the death,"* the Báb was killed on command of authority figures of Persia.

Therefore rejoice, ye heavens, and ye that dwell in them. Woe to the inhabiters of the earth and of the sea! for the devil is come down unto you, having great wrath, because he knoweth that he hath but a short time. (12)

Those within the heaven of spiritual renewal can enjoy salvation and the kingdom of God, but woe to those who indulge in the earth of past understanding and partake of the sea of severed concepts where confusion and disorder still reign. Little time remains for the devilish conditions of the past because the *"inhabiters of the earth"* are moving toward global understanding.

Preserving the Word of God

And when the dragon saw that he was cast unto the earth, he persecuted the woman which brought forth the man child. (13)

There have been many sacrifices and deaths for this new faith of God. The Bábí Faith, was rejected by the likes of the *"dragon,"* and suffered in its early years, beginning in 1844, persecution that resulted in as many as twenty thousand deaths and martyrs. Periodic suffering of the Bahá'í Faith within Persia has existed ever since.

And to the woman were given two wings of a great eagle, that she might fly into the wilderness, into her place, where she is nourished for a time, and times, and half a time, from the face of the serpent. (14)

This verse reverts back to the difficulties of early Islam (See commentary following vv. 12:3-4. The dragon and devil from the Pit of Error also perpetrated difficulties within Islam at that time. However, the Law of God was protected in the Arabian Peninsula for the duration of Islam. Many Muslims sincerely followed the verses of Muhammad, which were protected in His holy book, the Qur'an.

A *"time"* (year), and *"times"* (two years), and *"half a time"* (half year) are equal, by prophecy to 1260 days or years which is the duration of the Islamic Cycle and terminated by the coming of the Báb. Refer to Appendix for more details.

And the serpent cast out of his mouth water as a flood after the woman, that he might cause her to be carried away of the flood. (15)

Enemies of Islam, in pursuit of political power, jeered the spiritual message of Muhammad hoping to destroy the authority and power of the Word of God.

And the earth helped the woman, and the earth opened her mouth, and swallowed up the flood which the dragon cast out of his mouth. (16)

Inherent understanding among the followers of Muhammad living within the Hijaz Desert and Arabian Peninsula had power to dismiss the ignoble tirade of its enemies.

And the dragon was wroth with the woman, and went to make war with the remnant of her seed, which keep the commandments of God, and have the testimony of Jesus Christ. (17)

The woman represents the Law of God descended upon Muhammad, and the dragon persecuted her for the duration of the Islamic dispensation. The dragon at the end of the dispensation makes war *"with the remnant of her seed."* This occurrence refers to conditions surrounding the treatment and persecution of the Báb and Bahá'u'lláh and their followers by Persian authorities.

Revelation Chapter 13

World of the Beasts

And I stood upon the sand of the sea, and saw a beast rise up out of the sea, having seven heads and ten horns, and upon his horns ten crowns, and upon his heads the name of blasphemy. (1)

John sees a beast rise from a sea of dissension surrounding the revelation of Muhammad. The home of the beast is with the Umayyads. Collectively, kings and rulers of the Umayyad Dynasty become the beast and dragon. This dynasty gained control of Islam within about three decades of Muhammad's death.

> The beast that ascendeth out of the bottomless pit... means the Umayyads who attacked...from the pit of error, and who rose against the religion of Muhammad and against the reality of Alí - in other words, the love of God.[58]

As regards the beast, some verses are applicable to the Umayyads as a controlling power within Islam, while others seem compatible with the leaders of the Umayyads; particularly, in reference to their position as dignitaries representing the Faith of Muhammad. In either description the beast comes through as lacking a love for God.

The mystery of the *"seven heads and ten horns, and ... ten crowns"* is explained as follows: Political leaders from the tribe of the Umayyads ruled Seven Islamic territories, noted in 12:3, p. 122. Each of the heads carried the name of blasphemy. In verse 12:3 the dragon had seven crowns; one crown was allocated to each head of the seven territories. In verse 13:1 one crown is allocated to each of the ten names (horns) of the beast. There were ten different names, without repetition, of the fifteen different leaders in the Umayyad Dynasty.

---

[58] Ibid, p. 51.

And the beast which I saw was like unto a leopard, and his feet were as the feet of a bear, and his mouth as the mouth of a lion: and the dragon gave him his power, and his seat, and great authority. (2)

The leopard, bear, and lion represent metaphoric features of the beast, either as persons, political groups, or countries of the seven territories of Islam. These regions received power from members of the Umayyad Dynasty, i.e., those individual rulers as named by the explanation of verse 12:3. This dynasty represents the great red dragon with evil qualities of the serpent, Devil, and Satan. See Verse 12:9, p. 124.

And I saw one of his heads as it were wounded to death; and his deadly wound was healed: and all the world wondered after the beast. (3)

Evidence suggests that Alí , Muhammad's son-in-law, was the chosen leader of Islam following the death of Muhammad in 632 AD.[59] And historians do recognize Alí as the first spiritual leader. But not until his peers did acclaim him fourth caliph in 656 AD did Alí hold a position of political leadership. He was until his death in 661 AD both the first Imam and fourth Caliph.

Mu'áwíyah refused to give up his previous appointment as Governor of Syria when Alí became the fourth Caliph. A struggle for leadership, because of this disobedient action, led to Civil war within Islam. Dissatisfaction over this civil strife caused a group known as Seceders into a plot with intentions of killing Mu'áwíyah, Alí, and the governor of Egypt, Amr. These assassinations they felt would calm the warring factions of Islam. The action on 27 January 661 AD resulted in the death of Alí, and wounding of Mu'áwíyah from which he recovered.[60]

And they worshipped the dragon which gave power unto the beast: and they worshipped the beast, saying, Who is like unto the beast? who is able to make war with him? (4)

[59] Moojan Momen, *An Introduction to Shi'I Islam*, George Ronald, Oxford, Chapter 1.
[60] H.M. Balyuzi, *Muhammad and the Course of Islam*, George Ronald, Oxford, p.187.

The time of the dragon, Umayyad control, was the period of Islamic conquest. Its power was without comparison. In less then a century, the Umayyads conquered a territory from Spain to India, p. 92.

And there was given unto him a mouth speaking great things and blasphemies; and power was given unto him to continue forty and two months. (5)

The Umayyad Dynasty took on the attributes of a dragon and was protected by a religious covering of the Islamic State from which it blasphemed the teachings of Muhammad, v. 11:7, p. 110. The Umayyads and Muhammad belonged to the Quraysh tribe but to different clans; these were the House of Umayya and the House of Háshím.

The Islamic dispensation lasted for forty-two months or 1260 lunar years see Appendix, the period from 622 AD to 1844 AD. Control of state transferred from the Umayyads to the 'Abbásids and then to the Ottomans.

And he opened his mouth in blasphemy against God, to blaspheme his name, and his tabernacle, and them that dwell in heaven. (6)

The behavior of the Umayyads, though Islam was nominally a theocracy, debased the teachings of Muhammad and led to political control of State by this faction. Influence carried on throughout the centuries, v. 11:9, p. 111, so that, speaking of 19th-Century Persia:

> The people among whom He [the Báb] appeared were the most decadent race in the civilized world, grossly ignorant, savage, cruel, steeped in prejudice, servile in their submission to an almost deified hierarchy, recalling in their abjectness the Israelites of Egypt in the days of Moses, in their fanaticism the Jews in the days of Jesus, and in their perversity the idolaters of Arabia in the days of Muhammad.[61]

---

[61] Shoghi Effendi, *God Passes By*, Bahá'í Publishing Trust, Wilmette, Illinois, p. 4.

And it was given unto him to make war with the saints, and to overcome them: and power was given him over all kindreds, and tongues, and nations. (7)

Mu'áwíyah usurped Islamic power from the rightful heirs of Muhammad's Teachings. He made the Caliphate hereditary to his family that had from the beginning persecuted Muhammad and His followers. He and his son, Yazíd, who followed him as leader, were cause for the death of many of Muhammad's followers and relatives.

The politics of Islam developed from this beginning and included the kindreds, tongues and nations of its empire.

And all that dwell upon the earth shall worship him, whose names are not written in the book of life of the Lamb slain from the foundation of the world. (8)

"All that dwell upon the earth," without spiritual insight, *"whose names are not written in the book of life of the Lamb," "shall worship him,"* the beast. Mu'áwíyah controlled the Islamic State, created an Islamic legacy for his family, and passed on leadership to his son Yazíd. This control continued until the state was taken over by the 'Abbásids.

If any man have an ear, let him hear. He that leadeth into captivity shall go into captivity: he that killeth with the sword must be killed with the sword. Here is the patience and the faith of the saints. (9-10)

Those who hear must reflect. Progress of the saints, following recognition of their Lord, is through righteous behavior and works. Advancement, at times, appears very slow, and those who work for the Cause of God need much patience. Still, unity of purpose and righteous behavior are the only positive qualities that lead to social and spiritual improvement.

And I beheld another beast coming up out of the earth; and he had two horns like a lamb, and he spake as a dragon. (11)

Yazíd, the son of Mu'áwíyah , succeeded his father and gave continuity to the reign of the beast. Yazíd arose from the earth of Islamic politics—as opposed to a sea of spiritual considerations. The Caliphate had become hereditary to the Umayyads when Mu'áwíyah appointed Yazíd as his successor. Leaders became "caliphs" and "heirs" and therefore had two horns (names). The two horns are compared to a lamb as the Muslim leaders operated under the aegis of a theocracy.

Alternatively, the second beast can be interpreted as being the 'Abbásid Dynasty that fought for, and won control of the Islamic State.[62] Awareness of individuals and dynasties are both important to understanding the development and conditions of the Islamic State.

And he exerciseth all the power of the first beast before him, and causeth the earth and them which dwell therein to worship the first beast, whose deadly wound was healed. (12)

Usurpation of power by Mu'áwíyah gave political ascendancy unto the leaders of the Umayyad Clan. Clan members, as enemies of Muhammad, had opposed Him at Mecca and later fought Him at Medina. The most famous battle in Medina, before the era of Mu'áwíyah, was known as the Battle of the Trench; as many as ten thousand warriors fought against Muhammad and His followers.

During his reign, Yazíd worshipped the first beast and carried-forth political priorities initiated by his father. Patterns of behavior established by the Umayyads influenced many aspects of the full Islamic Dispensation. As an example, their successors, the 'Abbásids mirrored forth the behavior of the Umayyads. A leader of the newly formed 'Abbásid Dynasty, the governor of Syria, upon gaining control of the Islamic State invited some notable members of the Umayyads to a banquet. The Umayyads assumed amnesty, but during this event ninety of them were murdered.[63] 'Abda'r -Raymán escaped with his life. He it was who started an Umayyad Dynasty in Spain. In later centuries there developed numerous Islamic factions.

---

[62] Robert F. Riggs, *The Apocalypse Revealed*, Philosophical Library, New York, p. 168.
[63] H.M. Balyuzi, *Muhammad and the Course of Islam,* George Ronald, Oxford, p. 219.

And he doeth great wonders, so that he maketh fire come down from heaven on the earth in the sight of men, And deceiveth them that dwell on the earth by the means of those miracles which he had power to do in the sight of the beast; saying to them that dwell on the earth, that they should make an image to the beast, which had the wound by a sword, and did live. (13-14)

Yazíd's fame prior to becoming Caliph was partly because he had commanded an attack against Constantinople. On becoming Caliph his conduct, an image of his father, continued. His father, Mu'áwíyah, was indirect cause for Alí's death, and now Yazíd was the cause for death of Alí's youngest son, Husayn.

When Yazíd assumed power following Mu'áwíyah's death, loyal followers of Muhammad encouraged Husayn to rectify the situation. Mu'áwíyah's original agreement with Hasan, eldest son of Muhammad, allowed that following Mu'áwíyah's death, Islamic authority should revert to relatives of Muhammad. Hasan died some eight years later in 669 A.D. Now, with Mu'áwíyah's death, Husayn was, according to the agreement, the logical inheritor. Following encouragement by the faithful, Husayn, with a small contingent of about 70 members[64] excluding women and small children, set out for Kúfah to meet Yazíd. A commander, Al Hurr, who had command of a thousand men, intercepted Husayn. However, because of feelings of loyalty and compassion for Husayn, Al Hurr abandoned, along with thirty others, his men and post and joined ranks with Husayn. A second commander with a force of four thousand men was sent by Yazíd to replace Al Hurr. After unsuccessful negotiations, sporadic battle ensued and led to the death of Husayn, Al Hurr, and most all of the original contingent except for Husayn's sister and young son, Alí, who had been running a high fever at the time of battle. Husayn's head was decapitated, placed on a spear, and carried from city to city as a symbol of support for Yazíd.

The martyrdom of Husayn was a watershed in the development of Islamic history, and placed emphasis on the separation between the Shí'ah and Sunní Sects. Within Shí'ah Islam the episode is memorialized throughout the year, especially in the Month of Muharram; they are carried on from home celebrations to elaborate street processions that consist of ritualized

---

[64] Ibid, p. 194.

funeral processions and all of these events commemorate the suffering and martyrdom of Imam Husayn. Ignored by the Sunní Sect, these commemorations preserve hatred and resentment against the Sunnís.[65]

When Yazíd's massacre of Husayn's party at Karbilá became known, it caused a revolt in Medina. Yazíd sent an army under command of Muslim Ibn 'Uqbah to defeat the uprising. Crushing the revolt led to the Battle of Harrah when eighty companions of Muhammad and seven hundred Readers (those who had memorized the Qur'án) were massacred. "The city of the Prophet was given over to rapine: the barbarity displayed and the desecration wrought was past belief."[66]

And he had power to give life unto the image of the beast, that the image of the beast should both speak, and cause that as many as would not worship the image of the beast should be killed. And he causeth all, both small and great, rich and poor, free and bond, to receive a mark in their right hand, or in their foreheads: And that no man might buy or sell, save he that had the mark, or the name of the beast, or the number of his name. (15-17)

"No man might buy or sell, save he that had the mark, or the name of the beast, or the number of his name." Power of the Islamic state was supreme. Control of state, with specifics that depended on time and location, was reflected in policies of taxation, which varied over the course of Islam. Muhammad allowed Christians and Jews, People of the Book, to retain their religious beliefs even though being conquered. However, because they could not fight for Islam they were required to pay a poll or head tax, Jizyah. There was also a land tax, Kharaj. Pagans were not people of the book and, seemingly, suffered spiritual death unless they accepted Islam.

Here is wisdom. Let him that hath understanding count the number of the beast: for it is the number of a man; and his number is Six hundred threescore and six. (18)

Mu'áwíyah rejected Alí 's claim to position of caliph, and was indirectly the cause of Alí 's death. He became caliph in 661 AD, initiated the reign of

[65] Moojan Momen, *An Introduction to Shi'I Islam,* George Ronald, Oxford, p. 240.
[66] H.M. Balyuzi, *Muhammad and the Course of Islam,* George Ronald, Oxford, p.197.

the Umayyads, made successorship hereditary to his family, and defended his position by any possible means. He initiated the beastly reign. Why is his number 666? One explanation accounts for difficulties of chronology, which makes it possible, that the year 661 AD was in reality 666 AD.

Another possible reason follows from a need to widen his base of support because those who were spiritually close to Muhammad rejected Mu'áwíyah's claim to office. Therefore, in the early years of his Caliphate, Mu'áwíyah fostered numerous elements of self-serving deception in order to counter opposition from the believers in Medina and Mecca. He fomented fabrication of traditions ascribed to Muhammad in order to vilify Alí, instituted a daily ritual of cursing Him from the pulpit, and bribed subordinates to promote corruption of doctrine, text, belief and practice in order to further promote his own ends.[67] These actions must have carried on into the early years of his Caliphate, and possibly centered on the year 666 AD. Or, perhaps the symmetry of this number is ideal for its symbolic meaning. In any event, as noted in Verses 11:7, p. 110, the Umayyads are the beast; the chief antagonists of Muhammad's family were Mu'áwíyah and His son Yazíd.

---

[67] Ibid, p.192.

Proclaiming the Word

Chapters 14-16

Verily I say, this is the Day in which mankind can behold the Face, and hear the Voice, of the Promised One. The Call of God hath been raised, and the light of His countenance hath been lifted up upon men. It behoveth every man to blot out the trace of every idle word from the tablet of his heart, and to gaze, with an open and unbiased mind, on the signs of His Revelation, the proofs of His Mission, and the tokens of His glory.

Proclamation of Bahá'u'lláh, p. 111

Revelation Chapter 14

Everlasting Gospel

And I looked, and, lo, a Lamb stood on the mount Sion, and with him an hundred forty and four thousand, having his Father's name written in their foreheads. And I heard a voice from heaven, as the voice of many waters, and as the voice of a great thunder: and I heard the voice of harpers harping with their harps: And they sung as it were a new song before the throne, and before the four beasts, and the elders: and no man could learn that song but the hundred and forty and four thousand, which were redeemed from the earth. (1-3)

John saw a Lamb standing on God's holy mountain, Mount Sion. A figurative number of one hundred and forty four thousand followers, as previously prophesied in Chapter 7, were with Him. They are sealed: they are conscious of new Revelation, aware of the name of the Lamb's Father, and attracted to His qualities and teachings. Living in the time of the third woe, they are followers of Bahá'u'lláh Who was previously referenced in Verses 11:14-17. The name, Bahá'u'lláh , in Arabic means Glory of God, and, Bahá'í, means follower of Bahá. Bahá'u'lláh appears in the station of the Father; His titles, fulfilling prophecy, are many, p. 54.

> that what is meant in the prophecies by the 'Lord of Hosts' and the 'Promised Christ' is the Blessed Perfection (Bahá'u'lláh) and His holiness the Exalted One (the Báb).[68]

Since the Báb and Bahá'u'lláh, though of two separate dispensations, share in fulfillment of prophecy as to the promised Christ, the Lamb, we might expect, would be 'Abdu'l-Bahá Who shared a sacrificial forty years of banishment with Bahá'u'lláh. However the Lamb could be the Báb because He suffered the ultimate sacrifice in His martyrdom and also anticipated the building of the Kingdom of the Father through the Revelation of Bahá'u'lláh. The importance of the above verses, the author believes, is that

---

[68] Shoghi Effendi, *The World Order of Bahá'u'lláh,* Bahá'í Publishing Trust, Wilmette, Illinois p 139.

they, consistent with Chapter 11 as noted above, refer to the Revelation of Bahá'u'lláh Who is identified with the period of the third woe.

John hears the authoritative voice of Bahá'u'lláh, which has the sound of many spiritual waters (many prophets) and of great thunder. Only His followers can sing a new song of understanding in response to the heavenly setting of throne, beasts, elders, and spiritual awareness.

Followers of the Lamb

These are they which were not defiled with women; for they are virgins. These are they which follow the Lamb whithersoever he goeth. These were redeemed from among men, being the firstfruits unto God and to the Lamb. And in their mouth was found no guile: for they are without fault before the throne of God. (4-5)

In these verses, the Lamb refers to the Prophet because in each age and with each renewal of religion it is the Prophet Who speaks for God; those who believe not in His claims usually persecute him. His early followers are those who have singled out religious truth, possess material detachment, discovered the Prophet and Lamb of a new age, and abide by His teachings. God and His Prophet renew the spirit of mankind with support of new followers; apostles and adherents are, therefore, the first fruits unto God and the Lamb in a new dispensation. They carry forth His new teachings and have a spiritual legacy from all past religions. The followers respond to the Law of God and can be compared to early believers of Moses, Jesus Christ, Muhammad and other major Prophets.

Proclaiming a New Age

And I saw another angel fly in the midst of heaven, having the everlasting gospel to preach unto them that dwell on the earth, and to every nation, and kindred, and tongue, and people, Saying with a loud voice, Fear God, and give glory to him; for the hour of his judgment is come: and worship him that made heaven, and earth, and the sea, and the fountains of waters. (6-7)

The Báb opened this age in 1844 with new revelation declaring, with the strong voice of a trumpet blast, that all should fear God *"for the hour of his judgment is come,"* and that following His tenure, all people should worship "Him Whom God shall make Manifest,"[69] Bahá'u'lláh. God, through His

---

[69] Bahá'u'lláh, Kitáb-I-Aqdas, Bahá'í Publishing Trust, Wilmette, Illinois, Paragraph No. 135, p. 67.

Prophets, makes the *"heaven, and earth, and the sea, and the fountains of waters"* of spiritual understanding. Nineteen years following the declaration of the Báb, Bahá'u'lláh declared His mission. He renewed the Law of God by watering the earth of men's hearts with a sea of spiritual principles—eternal in the past and eternal in the future.

Babylon Shall Fall

And there followed another angel, saying, Babylon is fallen, is fallen, that great city, because she made all nations drink of the wine of the wrath of her fornication. And the third angel followed them, saying with a loud voice, If any man worship the beast and his image, and receive his mark in his forehead, or in his hand, The same shall drink of the wine of the wrath of God, which is poured out without mixture into the cup of his indignation; and he shall be tormented with fire and brimstone in the presence of the holy angels, and in the presence of the Lamb: And the smoke of their torment ascendeth up for ever and ever: and they have no rest day nor night, who worship the beast and his image, and whosoever receiveth the mark of his name. (8-11)

Contemporary with religious renewal comes the fall of the old order. In the last days, the great city of the past, as depicted in the Book of Revelation, is known as Babylon, which lacks spiritual verities in the conduct of its governance. For this reason, the past order is destined to fall. An explanation and warning is explained in the Bahá'í writings: while under banishment, Bahá'u'lláh wrote letters to Kings and Rulers of His age. In the *Promised Day is Come*, Bahá'u'lláh's great grandson, Shoghi Effendi, used many quotations from these letters and explains the historic significance of the downfall of kingdoms and dynasties. The following quotation provides an example:

What we witness at the present time, during 'this gravest crisis in the history of civilization,' recalling such times in which 'religions have perished and are born,' is the adolescent stage in the slow and painful evolution of humanity, preparatory to the attainment of the stage of manhood, the stage of maturity, the promise of which is embedded in the teachings, and enshrined in the prophecies, of Baha'u'llah. The tumult of this age of transition is characteristic of the impetuosity and irrational instincts of youth, its follies, its prodigality, its pride, its self-assurance, its rebelliousness, and contempt of discipline.[70]

During the transition phase, those who retain characteristics from out of the pit of error will suffer torment and remorse in the presence of those who follow the new teachings. Their anguish, they with the mark (fault) of the beast, *"ascendeth up forever and ever,"* and continues until such time as they are spiritually renewed.

Patience is Required

Here is the patience of the saints: here are they that keep the commandments of God, and the faith of Jesus. And I heard a voice from heaven saying unto me, Write, Blessed are the dead which die in the Lord from henceforth: Yea, saith the Spirit, that they may rest from their labours; and their works do follow them. (12-13)

Jesus Christ testifies, confirms the need for patience and blesses those who die in the Lord; they practice the principles enshrined within God's Word. They will rest and be rewarded for their labors as their works do follow them. In verses 6:9-10, p. 75, it was noted that opening of the fifth seal exposed many martyrs who worked for God's Cause in the past, these martyrs become impatient and want the Lord to judge and avenge their blood. Religious renewal has always suffered at the hands of vested powers, but new believers must keep the commandments of God, and keep the faith of Jesus.

Reaping the Clusters

And I looked, and behold a white cloud, and upon the cloud one sat like unto the Son of man, having on his head a golden crown, and in his hand a sharp sickle. And another angel came out of the temple, crying with a loud voice to him that sat on the cloud, Thrust in thy sickle, and reap: for the time is come for thee to reap; for the harvest of the earth is ripe. And he that sat on the cloud thrust in his sickle on the earth; and the earth was reaped. (14-16)

A Messenger of God who appeared *"like unto the Son of man,"* came on a white cloud (of purity) having in his hand the sharp sickle of the Word of God. He was a Prophet as indicated by his *"golden crown"* and prepared to initiate the religious process leading to renewal of the human spirit. *"And another angel"* from out of the temple informed Him, *"crying with a loud voice,"*

---

[70] Shoghi Effendi, *The Promised Day is Come,* Bahá'í Publishing Trust, Wilmette, Illinois, p. 121.

it is time to reap, i.e., to begin the process of renewal *"for the harvest of the earth is ripe."* These angels initiate the age, which fulfills prophecies concerning the return of Jesus.

Proclaiming the Word

And another angel came out of the temple which is in heaven, he also having a sharp sickle. And another angel came out from the altar, which had power over fire; and cried with a loud cry to him that had the sharp sickle, saying, Thrust in thy sharp sickle, and gather the clusters of the vine of the earth; for her grapes are fully ripe. And the angel thrust in his sickle into the earth, and gathered the vine of the earth, and cast it into the great winepress of the wrath of God. (17-19)

In the metaphoric comparison of the juice of the grape to the spirit of the Word, there lies a need in either case for extraction. With the former it is the ordinary squeeze of the winepress and with the latter it is the pressure of the winepress of the wrath of God that is applied. This pressure, according to the authors understanding, is associated with the process of proclaiming the Word of God, an inherent need of all new revelation

'Abdu'l-Bahá was a champion of the Revelation of the third woe. In His words, "As to my station, it is that of the servant of Bahá; 'Abdu'l-Bahá, the visible expression of servitude to the Threshold of the Abha Beauty."[71] He possessed angelic power and complete understanding of his Father's teachings, the Word of God, p. 20. He had been sanctioned by Bahá'u'lláh to proclaim the Faith—the grapes, or spirit of new teachings, were ripe. Bahá'u'lláh is from the Temple and also from out of the altar, which is closest to God. His son, 'Abdu'l-Bahá, acting in the capacity of His station took the message of new revelation to various countries. He brought the everlasting gospel to Europe and America and announced that the Promised Day had come. On July 5, 1912, 'Abdu'l-Bahá opened a talk in New York City with the following words in regard to this age:

You are very welcome, very welcome, all of you! In the divine Holy Books there are unmistakable prophecies giving the glad tidings of a certain Day in which the Promised One of all the Books would appear, a radiant dispensation be established, the banner of the Most Great Peace and conciliation be hoisted and

---

[71] 'Abdu'l-Bahá, Selection from the Writings of 'Abdu'l-Bahá, Bahá'í World Center, Haifa, Israel, p 56.

the oneness of the world of humanity proclaimed. Among the various nations and peoples of the world no enmity or hatred should remain. All hearts were to be connected one with another. These things are recorded in the Torah, or Old Testament, in the Gospel, the Qur'an, the Zend-Avesta, the books of Buddha and the book of Confucius. In brief, all the Holy Books contain these glad tidings. They announce that after the world is surrounded by darkness, radiance shall appear. For just as the night, when it becomes excessively dark, precedes the dawn of a new day, so likewise when the darkness of religious apathy and heedlessness overtakes the world, when human souls become negligent of God, when materialistic ideas overshadow spirituality, when nations become submerged in the world of matter and forget God - at such a time as this shall the divine Sun shine forth and the radiant morn appear.[72]

Prophet-Revelators represent the true vine of the earth. "I am the true vine, and my Father is the husbandman." (John 15:1). Humanity learns the lessons of spirituality from the fruit of this vine. When Jesus spoke of His second coming he said, "But I say unto you, I will not drink henceforth of this fruit of the vine, until that day when I drink it new with you in my Father's kingdom." (Mat 26:29) The Spirit of the scriptures would be renewed at that time in the Father's kingdom. Those who refuse spiritual renewal and remain attached to the qualities of the depraved beasts must suffer deprivation of spirit until they drink from the wine of renewal, which is a bounty from God and His winepress.

The Spirit is Drained

And the winepress was trodden without the city, and blood came out of the winepress, even unto the horse bridles, by the space of a thousand and six hundred furlongs. (20)

In preparation for renewal, *"without the city,"* pressing of the vine brings forth the blood of its fruit or spirit, even to the bridle of control and direction. All peoples must eventually succumb to the reordering of the future.

---

[72] 'Abdu'l-Bahá, *Promulgation of Universal Peace,* Bahá'í Publishing Trust, Wilmette, Illinois, p. 215-216.

Revelation Chapter 15

Seven Last Plagues

And I saw another sign in heaven, great and marvellous, seven angels having the seven last plagues; for in them is filled up the wrath of God. (1)

The subject of the winepress metaphor continues in a new way. Seven *"great and marvelous"* angelic powers of God shall call out the path of spiritual renewal; their message is sent as a bounty of God. Those who reject the message, and suffer from deprivation, must experience the consequence of their own denial. The immediate social environment is a result of their behavior. As previously noted, revelation comes at a time of great difficulty and is referenced by scriptural verses as a period of woe. Troubles of this period are prolonged while those who hear the Word reject its message of spiritual renewal.

Angels of Renewal

And I saw as it were a sea of glass mingled with fire: and them that had gotten the victory over the beast, and over his image, and over his mark, and over the number of his name, stand on the sea of glass, having the harps of God. (2)

Every revelation has its immediate followers who promote the process of spiritual renewal. With this Revelation, it is those who had gotten the victory over the 19th-Century beast and beyond. Those who overcome, p. 54, stand on a firm footing mingled with fire of the love of God before His throne in heaven as noted in verse 4:6, p. 60. Heaven is a spiritual state that can be achieved in earthly life, or in the dimension of life after death. It is nearness to God in either case.

Sing the Song of Renewal

And they sing the song of Moses the servant of God, and the song of the Lamb, saying, Great and marvellous are thy works, Lord God Almighty; just and true are thy ways, thou King of saints. (3)

All sincere believers in God *"sing the song of Moses...and of the Lamb,"* display the qualities of servant and recognize the need for spiritual renewal and personal sacrifice. They feel God's methods are *"just and true."*

> Consider Moses! Armed with the rod of celestial dominion, adorned with the white hand of Divine knowledge, and proceeding from the Paran [A reference to Muhammad and the Arabs.] of the love of God, and wielding the serpent of power and everlasting majesty, He shone forth from the Sinai of light upon the world. He summoned all the peoples and kindreds of the earth to the kingdom of eternity, and invited them to partake of the fruit of the tree of faithfulness.[73]

Because of the Prophets, social laws are restated to meet the exigencies of the age and spiritual laws are reactivated without change. Followers of this revelation see God's Cause as a continuing process encountering periodic renewals and show highest respect for the Eternal Father and His Prophets.

Nations Shall Worship

Who shall not fear thee, O Lord, and glorify thy name? for thou only art holy: for all nations shall come and worship before thee; for thy judgments are made manifest. (4)

This is the age in which nations will assume spiritual qualities, as reflected in verse 2:26, p. 56, a factor in support of a peaceful society and the unity of nations. Submission to God's judgment, tantamount to recognition of His sovereignty, and practice of the Law of God for this age becomes the standards for a new era and represents fear and glorification of His name.

> Rest thou assured that in this era of the spirit, the Kingdom of Peace will raise up its tabernacle on the summits of the world, and the commandments of the Prince of Peace will so dominate the arteries and nerves of every people as to draw into His sheltering shade all the nations on earth.[74]

---

[73] Bahá'u'lláh, *Gleanings from the Writings of Bahá'u'lláh*, Bahá'í Publishing Trust, Wilmette, Illinois, p 19.
[74] 'Abdu'l-Bahá, *Selection from the Writings of 'Abdu'l-Bahá*, Bahá'í World Center, Haifa, Israel, p. 246.

Testimony for Renewal

And after that I looked, and, behold, the temple of the tabernacle of the testimony in heaven was opened: And the seven angels came out of the temple, having the seven plagues, clothed in pure and white linen, and having their breasts girded with golden girdles. (5-6)

Seven angels from out of the sanctuary of heavenly testimony wore garments of purity and golden girdles of spiritual authority. They shall make known the essentials of proclamation during the early phase of religious renewal. Persecution and banishment of the Prophet and some of His immediate followers typifies the response of past leaders. These events provide further testimony about the authenticity of God's Cause; continuing radiance of the Prophet under these trying conditions of persecution is one of the confirmations to the truth of His Revelation.

Final Preparation

And one of the four beasts gave unto the seven angels seven golden vials full of the wrath of God, who liveth for ever and ever. (7)

One of the friendly beasts gives a *"golden vial"* to each of the seven angels. The author understands these golden flasks contain valuable matter aligned with early experiences of a new age. Release of this matter is a bounty from God to those who overcome and recognize the Prophet but is seen as wrath from the viewpoint of those who reject the message.

And the temple was filled with smoke from the glory of God, and from his power; and no man was able to enter into the temple, till the seven plagues of the seven angels were fulfilled. (8)

The temple, representing a collective center, p. 46, of God and His Revelator, is filled *"from the glory of God, and from his power,"* (emphasis added) and portrays the fire of the word as renewed; spiritual renewal requires a change in the behavior of people and, for dissenters, often leads to controversy and the arising smoke of conflict. As regards the above verse, Bahá'ís often refer to it as being a reference to Bahá'u'lláh Whose name means the glory, the light and the splendor of God.[75] (See also verse 21:22, p. 200.) In His words:

> We have caused the rivers of Divine utterance to proceed out of Our throne, that the tender herbs of wisdom and understanding may spring forth from the soil of your hearts. Will ye not be thankful? They who disdain to worship their Lord shall be of those who are cast off. And oft as Our verses are rehearsed unto them, they persist in proud disdain, and in their gross violation of His law, and know it not. As for them who have disbelieved in Him, they shall be in the shadow of a black smoke. 'The Hour' hath come upon them, while they are disporting themselves. They have been seized by their forelock, and yet know it not.[76]

No man can enter the Cause of God, the temple, until its new message has been fully disclosed. The early years of the Bábí and Bahá'í Faiths representing the initial phase of proclamation are briefly reviewed in the next chapter.

---

[75] Shoghi Effendi, *God Passes By,* Bahá'í Publishing Trust, Wilmette, Illinois, p. 94.
[76] Bahá'u'lláh, *Gleanings from the Writings of Bahá'u'lláh,* Bahá'í Publishing Trust, Wilmette, Illinois, p. 43.

Revelation Chapter 16

Process Begins

And I heard a great voice out of the temple saying to the seven angels, Go your ways, and pour out the vials of the wrath of God upon the earth. (1)

John heard the voice of God announce to the powers of renewal, seven angels, it was time for spiritual restoration. They are told to deliver their message; it must make connections with the hearts of people and institutions of the social environment.

As regards the characteristics of angels, 'Abdu'l-Bahá has stated, "God's confirming power shineth out from the lamp-niche of [their] souls."[77] We conclude they are highly developed spiritually, and also, as noted by Ruth J. Moffett,[78] He states that the seven angels represent seven powers. Therefore, this author understands them as seven spiritual powers, or vehicles of whatever form, commissioned to deliver the message of renewal in what is known as the Heroic Age. Their message, because of some conflict with tradition, elicits various responses, and where wrath is involved, the recipients reject the Word and sustain existing social disturbances. In the following explanation about the Bábí Faith, religious and political leaders actively reject the Prophet's revelation.

> The judgment of God, so rigorous and unsparing in its visitations on those who took a leading or an active part in the crimes committed against the Báb and His followers, was not less severe in its dealings with the mass of the people ... From the very day the hand of the assailant was stretched forth against the Báb ... visitation upon visitation crushed the spirit out of that ungrateful people, and brought them to the very brink of national bankruptcy. Plagues, the very names of which were almost unknown to them except for

---

[77] 'Abdu'l-Bahá, *Selections from the Writings of 'Abdu'l-Bahá,* Bahá'í World Center, Haifa, Israel, p.166.
[78] Ruth J. Moffett, *New Keys to the Book of Revelation,* Bahá'í Publishing Trust, New Delhi, India, p. 93-94.

a cursory reference in the dust-covered books which few cared to read, fell upon them with a fury that none could escape.[79]

The early history of the Bábí and Bahá'í Faiths in its Heroic Age suffers from the most extreme forms of persecution, and outwardly, it is this response that incurs God's wrath. Presented terminology of wrath is applicable to the Heroic Age of the Faith, but later all humanity, the entire globe will most likely experience the pull toward renewal. Many people of this age feel, as a follow on to a century of world and ideological wars, a generally deteriorating world condition in need of renewal. Much discontent about the current environment exists and, more and more, a need for resurrection of the human spirit is seen.

Challenge to Understanding

And the first went, and poured out his vial upon the earth; and there fell a noisome and grievous sore upon the men which had the mark of the beast, and upon them which worshipped his image. (2)

Challenged by the first vial, it is discovered those who associate with the beast share his beastly qualities. With the formation of the Sunní Caliphate, Islam became a mix of politics and religion, and Umayyad Caliphs, original enemies of Muhammad, influenced the course of Islam. Present day leaders of similar religious and political understanding, having positions of power and control, are reluctant to hear the Word of God, because it interferes with their sense of equity. They are therefore the cause for persecution of the Prophet and His followers. Only through spiritual rebirth and enlightened understanding does the human heart seek to renew human virtues and cure spiritual wounds.

Challenge to Behavior

And the second angel poured out his vial upon the sea; and it became as the blood of a dead man; and every living soul died in the sea. (3)

Next, the sea of behavior is questioned and shown to contain the spirit of a dead man, and all those partaking thereof had died. This challenge is in response to a vast reservoir of idle fancies originating because of deviation from meaning of the written Word. Such beliefs come from vain imagin-

---

[79] Shoghi Effendi, *God Passes By,* Bahá'í Publishing Trust, Wilmette, Illinois, pp. 84-85.

ings, are subjectively inspired, and ordinarily have material attachments without social value leading to social injustice and unrest.

Throughout the world, social disturbances continue, even into the new millennium. The sea of dissension and disunity has become as the life force or *"blood of a dead man."*

Challenge to Authorities

And the third angel poured out his vial upon the rivers and fountains of waters; and they became blood. (4)

The third angel questioned the contributions from spiritual sources, noted as rivers and fountains of waters. Leaders who operate at this level sometime support dictates from the sea of idle fancies and remain indoctrinated with the status quo of tradition and uncontrolled institutional power. Original spiritual power paralyzed by the legacy of the beast then becomes as the blood (spirit) of the dead.

And I heard the angel of the waters say, Thou art righteous, O Lord, which art, and wast, and shalt be, because thou hast judged thus. (5)

The authority of the waters acknowledged that the Lord is righteous in making judgments in relation to past spiritual operations. With authority and power from knowledge of reality, he confirms the need for corrections to the spiritual waters. The eternal God has judged righteously in sending His angels of renewal to the practitioners of political and religious understanding and their institutions.

For they have shed the blood of saints and prophets, and thou hast given them blood to drink; for they are worthy. (6)

Spiritual authority combined with unrealistic understanding has been cause for persecution of saints and Prophets. This verse suggests that the keepers of the waters are worthy (by station) to have the life force of blood (spirit) to drink, or, conversely for some, they deserve the fate of a dead man because of shedding *"the blood of saints and prophets."*

And I heard another out of the altar say, Even so, Lord God Almighty, true and right-
eous are thy judgments. (7)

A power, closest to God, confirmed the righteousness of God's judgments. Even though religious leaders are perceived as role models, the
judgments of God are righteous; the clergy as a group for lack of recognition of the Prophets have not only cast the Word in frozen doctrine according to their own understanding but have also persecuted those Prophets
who have come to renew the Word of God. Unrecognized grace of the
Holy Spirit in the day of the Prophet leads to the torment of unbelief.

Message to Persia

And the fourth angel poured out his vial upon the sun; and power was given unto him to
scorch men with fire. (8)

The revelation of the Báb was initiated in Persia whose emblem is the
sun. Power of the fourth angel inspired many of the people with the fire of
the love of God. In the early days of this occurrence, during a forty-day
period, eighteen persons independently discovered the Báb. These dignitaries, equivalent of disciples, along with the Báb constituted the Nineteen
Letters of the Living and were recognized by 'Abdu'l-Bahá as the Elders of
the Book of Revelation before the throne of God, p. 60.

During the Báb's pilgrimage to the foremost holy cities of Islam, Mecca
and Medina, His disciples had elicited within Persia a positive response
from many of the people. "The fire which the declaration of His mission
had lit was being fanned into flame through the dispersal and activities of
His appointed disciples."[80] Upon His return and magnified by His own
proclamations, "Siyyids of distinguished merit, eminent 'ulamás, and even
government officials were boldly and rapidly espousing the Cause."[81] So
great was the excitement that an inveterate enemy, the Shí'ah clergy, sanctioned by sovereigns of the Qájár dynasty, arranged that the Báb should be
tried for heresy. The direction of this investigation became favorable to the
Báb and, to the chagrin of His adversaries, gave him opportunity to proclaim "before a distinguished assembly in Tabris, the capital of Ádhirbáy-
ján."[82]

---

[80] Ibid, p. 10.
[81] Ibid, p. 20
[82] Ibid, p. 33.

And men were scorched with great heat, and blasphemed the name of God, which hath power over these plagues: and they repented not to give him glory. (9)

And Persian leaders, under influence of existing institutions, were reluctant to change their ways. Calamitous events, whether coincidental or by Divine Providence, gave a brief spell of freedom to the Báb in the days of His impending imprisonment. Shoghi Effendi in *God Passes By* quotes the Báb regarding the response of His persecutors:

> 'Call thou to remembrance the early days of the Revelation. How great the number of those who died of cholera! That was indeed one of the prodigies of the Revelation, and yet none recognized it! During four years the scourge raged among Shi'ah Muslims without any one grasping its significance!' 'As to the great mass of its people (Persia),' Nabil has recorded in his immortal narrative *[The Dawn-Breakers]*, 'who watched with sullen indifference the tragedy that was being enacted before their eyes, and who failed to raise a finger in protest against the hideousness of those cruelties, they fell, in their turn, victims to a misery which all the resources of the land and the energy of its statesmen were powerless to alleviate'[83]

The Báb's message was given to fanatical leaders who had little insight about searching for or discovery of a Prophet of God. Understanding the weakness of their perspective, He was aware of His approaching martyrdom, and in preparing for the future continuity of His followers, He had forecast the coming of Bahá'u'lláh, which event would emerge 19 years following His own declaration. He wrote an exposition while imprisoned within the fortress of Máh-Kú called the Bayán. In this work He significantly speaks of the coming of Bahá'u'lláh. 'Well is it with him who fixeth his gaze upon the Order of Bahá'u'lláh, and rendereth thanks unto his Lord. For He will assuredly be made manifest.'[84]

After a six-year ministry in which the Báb questioned current perceptions of religious renewal, chastised spiritual misconceptions, and challenged the purveyors of religious thought, He suffered a martyrs death. His

---

[83] Shoghi Effendi, *God Passes By*, Bahá'í Publishing Trust, Wilmette, Illinois, pp. 84-85.
[84] Bahá'u'lláh, *Aqdas*, Bahá'í Publishing Trust, Wilmette, Illinois, Note 189, p. 245.

ministry led to an influx of many followers, their persecution, and in many cases their martyrdom. Some twenty thousand followers of the Báb were killed.

Wider Dispersion

And the fifth angel poured out his vial upon the seat of the beast; and his kingdom was full of darkness; and they gnawed their tongues for pain, And blasphemed the God of heaven because of their pains and their sores, and repented not of their deeds. (10-11)

Bahá'u'lláh had been imprisoned as a follower of the Báb in a dungeon in Tehran known as the Síyáh-Chál. Following His release He was banished to Baghdad, an early seat of Islam. His family, and some followers accompanied Him. It was while imprisoned in the Síyáh-Chál that Bahá'u'lláh first became aware of His true station; however, it would be more than another decade that He remained known as a Bábí. While in Baghdad and later, the uncovering of His Divine mission was continually hampered by the envious machinations of Yahyá, His half-brother, and one Siyyid Muhammad who historians have noted as being the antichrist of the Bahá'í Revelation. Until these issues were finally resolved, the covenant breakers at intervals attempted to discredit Him and usurp His rightful and God-given station as Prophet of God. The perpetrators of these corrupting affairs *"blasphemed the God of heaven,"* and *"repented not of their deeds."*

In order to avoid disunity during the early Baghdad period because of the deviant activities of Yahyá and his cohorts, Bahá'u'lláh separated Himself from His immediate family and friends disguised as a dervish and took a two-year sojourn in Kurdistan. He quietly departed and His whereabouts was for a long time unknown. In His absence, Yahyá and friends, by their activities, had ample time and free reign to demonstrate their mean-spirited purpose and scheming nature. These forces of personal gain and design, apparent to observers living in a leadership vacuum, caused further weakening of the Báb's followers both within Persia and among the exiled Bábís.

Bahá'u'lláh's spiritual qualities and profound knowledge were recognized while in Kurdistan; there He became a member of a distinguished group of religious scholars that recognized His qualities befitting a Prophet and there, by word and deed, He provided strong contributions to their spiritual perceptions. He relinquished His stay in that region only when discovered by one of His fellow exiles that pleaded for His return to the banished community.

Following His return to Baghdad, Bahá'u'lláh continued to gain greater recognition from certain government officials, especially of Iraq. This attention and others from visiting acquaintances He had met in Kurdistan led to growing prestige and strengthening of the Bábí Community. Observed by the rebellious, this turn of fortune, led to their sponsoring further schemes and dissensions. These difficulties in conjunction with more coercion from Persian officials precipitated the next leg of Bahá'u'lláh's banishment.

Shortly before leaving Baghdad following orders of further banishment, Bahá'u'lláh sojourned with His immediate followers on an island in the Tigris River named by Him the Garden of Ridván (Paradise). In this setting, He informed his immediate associates and many other friends during a 12-day period about His true station. The episode was highly charged emotionally and particularly difficult for those who would be left behind. This period, known as the Festival of Ridván, is now commemorated by Bahá'ís as the holiest Bahá'í celebration.

Spirit of Euphrates Dried Up

And the sixth angel poured out his vial upon the great river Euphrates; and the water thereof was dried up, that the way of the kings of the east might be prepared. (12)

The region of the Euphrates and Tigris Rivers had been home to early civilizations and conditioned by some of the great cultures and religions of the past. This influence reached a zenith under the integrating influence of the 'Abbásid Caliphate; essentially, all past knowledge of the Middle East was absorbed by them and later funneled to the Schoolmen of Western Europe and became the cause of much European progress. Beyond this high point of accomplishment learning and science in the Euphrates region ceased to advance, and ignorance prevailed, at least on a relative basis.

Material achievements, in those regions that employed modern scientific method, advanced rapidly in the Western World. And with the coming of the Revelations of the Báb and Bahá'u'lláh, of the second and third woes, cultural and spiritual renewal was being passed through the same corridor that had sustained ancient civilizations. Past cultural and spiritual influence—Jewish, Christian, Muslim and Zoroastrian[85]—had spent its allotted

---

[85] Hushidar Motlagh, *I Shall Come Again*, Global Perspective, Mt. Pleasant, Michigan, p. 306.

time, and now these waters were being dried up in preparation for worldwide spiritual renewal, pp. 47-48.

In the sense that scriptures refer to the Prophet as a spiritual King, drying up of the *"great river Euphrates"* in preparation *for "the way of the Kings of the east"* is understood to refer to the Faith of Bahá'u'lláh.

> Ye are but vassals, O kings of the earth! He Who is the King of Kings hath appeared, arrayed in His most wondrous glory, and is summoning you unto Himself, the Help in Peril, the Self-Subsisting.[86]

Reactionary Forces

And I saw three unclean spirits like frogs come out of the mouth of the dragon, and out of the mouth of the beast, and out of the mouth of the false prophet. For they are the spirits of devils, working miracles, which go forth unto the kings of the earth and of the whole world, to gather them to the battle of that great day of God Almighty. (13-14)

A devilish spirit has, at times, influenced the secular/political kings of the earth, and now forces of evil are gathering for that great day of God Almighty, the time when spiritual renewal prevails. Within the faith, the storm existed because of Yahyá. He had, in a figurative sense, been appointed chief of the Bábí's for the interim period until the Báb's true successor would become apparent. Not recognizing or admitting to this guise, Yahyá eventually went so far as to declare his own self as being the true successor to the Báb. Siyyid Muhammad had recognized this ambition within Yahyá and also became aware of being able to manipulate him toward the end of his own ambitions. Between the two of them, along with a few others, they became the driving force of a storm, which finally would be resolved in Adrianople. The dark clouds of this disturbance in its various forms existed primarily from the early days of Baghdad until banishment had taken the exiles to Adrianople, a period of about fourteen-years.

Partial Declaration

Behold, I come as a thief. Blessed is he that watcheth, and keepeth his garments, lest he walk naked, and they see his shame. (15)

---

[86] Bahá'u'lláh, Aqdas, Bahá'í Publishing Trust, Wilmette, Illinois, Paragraph 82, p. 50.

"The process whereby the effulgence of so dazzling a Revelation was unfolded to the eyes of men was of necessity slow and gradual. The first intimation which its Bearer received did not synchronize with, nor was it followed immediately by, a disclosure of its character to either His own companions or His kindred."[87] Bahá'u'lláh appeared nearly undetected, with the exception of the spiritually perceptive, until His declaration in the Garden of Ridván. The matter of declaring His mission had, as previously noted, centered to a considerable extent on the behavior of His half-brother, Yahyá, in conjunction with his friend, Siyyid Muhammad. Some Bábí's including the Siyyid had already observed Bahá'u'lláh's spiritual qualities and power of leadership following the martyrdom of the Báb. Arising jealousy within Siyyid Muhammad led him to discredit Bahá'u'lláh in so far as possible. Later this effort was reinforced when he discovered, for his purpose, a useful tool in Yahyá who had similar feelings about Bahá'u'lláh.

It was because of these forces, or those of Divine Destiny, that He made His station known only at propitious moments suitable to the needs of the Bábí Community at-large. In His own words He explains, "It must be evident to all that We did not accept calamities and did not become captive except for the glorification of the Cause of God and bearing witness to the truth of His Word."[88]

In reference to the covenant breakers, the sentiment of the above verse seems applicable; namely, that good behavior of any individual is appropriately blessed *"lest he walk naked, and they see his shame."*

Continuing Difficulties

And he gathered them together into a place called in the Hebrew tongue Armageddon. (16)

Disturbing forces within and without the community had now been cause "to transfer His residence to the center of still greater preeminence, the capital city of the Ottoman Empire, the seat of the Caliphate, the administrative center of Sunní Islam, the abode of the most powerful potentate in the Islamic world."[89] This stay in Constantinople (Istanbul) lasted but four months when an edict setting forth continued banishment to Adrianople was ordered by "Sultán 'Abdu'l-Azíz himself, the self-styled vicar of the Prophet of Islám and the absolute ruler of a mighty empire." The order

---

[87] Shoghi Effendi, *God Passes By*, Bahá'í Publishing Trust, Wilmette, Illinois, p. 103.

[88] Balyuzi, *Baha'u'llah, the King of Glory,* George Ronald, Oxford, p. 235

[89] Shoghi Effendi, *God Passes By*, Bahá'í Publishing Trust, Wilmette, Illinois, p. 145.

came "suddenly and without any justification whatsoever, in the depth of winter, and in the most humiliating circumstances..."[90]

The banished exiles would now experience "what is admittedly the most turbulent and critical period of the first Bahá'í century—a period that was destined to precede the most glorious phase of that ministry, the proclamation of His Message to the world and its rulers."[91]

The disruptions of Yahyá were about to reach a climax. He had in the past been cause for the murder of some well known Bábí's, disseminated falsified documents, and was now attempting to have Bahá'u'lláh murdered. This he attempted by poisoning, having a hired gun, and by encouraging an attendant to kill Him while at His service in the public bath. Each of these schemes was discovered and Yahyá was badly discredited. Siyyid Muhammad, who boasted that a face-to-face confrontation between Bahá'u'lláh and Yahyá was imminent, initiated the final blow to any remaining credibility. This meeting would be a battle to separate truth from error and is known in that culture as a mubáhilih. Following repeated attempts at a meeting, neither Yahyá nor Siyyid Muhammad made an appearance. Word of this shameful episode reached Persia and the Bábís, except for a few, had now come to recognize that Bahá'u'lláh was fulfillment of "He Whom God shall make manifest" as promised by the Báb.

Some close followers, even before His declaration in the Garden of Ridván, had apparently understood the true nature of Bahá'u'lláh's station and there was considerable additional awareness because of that declaration. Also, Bahá'u'lláh had written some of His best-known works in the Baghdad period and this aspect provided further observable evidence of His calling. He now while in Adrianople, and in part prior to resolution of the difficulties with Yahyá, felt compelled to communicate some of His most powerful messages.

Open Declaration

And the seventh angel poured out his vial into the air; and there came a great voice out of the temple of heaven, from the throne, saying, It is done. (17)

Just as all peoples partake of a common need for air, the seventh angel works for universal renewal of the spirit. Bahá'u'lláh's declaration had now

---

[90] Ibid, pp. 158-159.
[91] Ibid, p. 162.

become all encompassing. His mission is for the good of all people and essential to the well being of mankind. While in Adrianopole, "Day and night the Divine verses were raining down in such number that it was impossible to record them." "In those days the equivalent of all that hath been sent down aforetime unto the Prophets hath been revealed."[92] Among others, He addressed Tablets to contemporary political and religious leaders informing them of His mission and the more urgent contents of His message. In this period the phrase "the people of the Bayan," representing followers of Mirza Yahyá, was replaced by the term "the people of Baha."[93]

These successes, observable to the enemies of the Faith, once more precipitated another leg of banishment, which was initiated by the powers of the Ottoman government. When the officials had settled on new arrangements, Bahá'u'lláh was sent to the prison city of Acca, Palestine and Yahyá to Farmagusta, Cypress where he and some others were no longer in position to damage the Cause of God.

This process of banishment, intrigue, separation, and victory of good over evil, important as they were to the Faith, is believed to also exemplify those difficulties associated with adjustments required to achieve a unified and peaceful world. Difficulties of this age can be seen as the battle of Armageddon. What seems in the 20th-Century the ultimate expression of the wrath of God has been one of sustained warfare and international anarchy, a continuing piling on of troubles.[94] Humankind is gradually learning that wars do not solve social and cultural differences. The ultimate solution to the human predicament lies in recognition of the oneness of mankind, the acceptance of a diversified world, and acknowledgement of God's Prophet for this age of renewal. 'Abdu'l-Bahá has explained that humanity's singleness of purpose toward a global civilization will grow with the development of expressions of unity in politics, world undertakings, freedoms, religions, nations, races, and language.[95]

Armageddon is often viewed as one final battle. Metaphorically an earthquake of change or adjustments, the thundering of instructions, etc,

---

[92] Ibid, pp. 170-171.
[93] Ibid, p.176.
[94] Robert F. Riggs, *The Apocalypse Unsealed,* Philosophical Library, New York, p. 203.
[95] 'Abdu'l-Bahá, *Selections from the Writings of 'Abdu'l-Bahá,* Bahá'í Publishing Trust, Wilmette, Illinois, p 32.

characterizes it. Ruth J. Moffett[96] points out that this final battle is most likely composed of the Battle of Nations, the Economic Battle, the Political battle, the Battle of Disease, the Battle of the Forces of Nature, the Battle of the Races, and the Battle of Religions. All these struggles relate to essential issues in need of resolution on the road to formation of a unified and peaceful world.

The Responses

And there were voices, and thunders, and lightnings; and there was a great earthquake, such as was not since men were upon the earth, so mighty an earthquake, and so great. (18)

The metaphoric content of this verse is explained by reference to verse 11:15, 18, and 19. Both Chapters 11 and 16, in their latter verses, as interpreted, discuss the response of the people, whether as nations or individuals, to the spiritual and social changes mandated by religious renewal at the end of the Islamic dispensation.

The following quotations are taken from that source as noted:

> [T]he Book of His Testament will appear in His Jerusalem, the Epistle of the Covenant will be established, and the meaning of the Testament and of the Covenant will become evident. The renown of God will overspread the East and West, and the proclamation of the Cause of God will fill the world. The violators of the Covenant will be degraded and dispersed, and the faithful cherished and glorified, for they cling to the Book of the Testament and are firm and steadfast in the Covenant. (Third paragraph following 11:19.)

In respect to terminology such as *"lightnings"*, *"thunder,"* *"earthquake,"* and *"hail,"* 'Abdu'l-Bahá explains:

> [A]fter the appearance of the Book of the Testament there will be a great storm, and the lightnings of the anger and the wrath of God will flash, the noise of the thunder of the violation of the Covenant will resound, the earthquake of doubts will take place,

---

[96] Ruth J. Moffett, *New Keys to the Book of Revelation,* Bahá'í Publishing Trust, New Delhi, India, p. 99-100

the hail of torments will beat upon the violators of the Covenant, and even those who profess belief will fall into trials and temptations. (Last paragraph following 11:19.)

As to physical earthquakes, "About 50,000 earthquake large enough to be felt or noticed without the aid of instruments occur annually over the entire Earth. Of these approximately 100 are of sufficient size to produce substantial damage if their centers are near areas of habitation. Very great earthquakes occur at an average rate of about one per year."[97] It seems for interpretation of verses, the possibility of material earthquakes cannot be disregarded as an additional sign of the times.

The Prevailing Environment

And the great city was divided into three parts, and the cities of the nations fell: and great Babylon came in remembrance before God, to give unto her the cup of the wine of the fierceness of his wrath. (19)

Guidance of the people had been replaced by three ideologies of mankind. These must fall and be replaced by the City of God, which is the Law of God renewed. At a universal level that *"great city,"* the Law of God, must cherish for its Champion, the one True and Eternal God. However, as Shoghi Effendi has explained, the 20th-Century has been occupied with false gods and idle fancies:

> This vital force [Religion] is dying out, this mighty agency has been scorned, this radiant light obscured, this impregnable stronghold abandoned, this beauteous robe discarded. God Himself has indeed been dethroned from the hearts of men, and an idolatrous world passionately and clamorously hails and worships the false gods which its own idle fancies have fatuously created, and its misguided hands so impiously exalted. The chief idols in the desecrated temple of mankind are none other than the triple gods of Nationalism, Racialism and Communism, at whose altars governments and peoples, whether democratic or totalitarian, at peace or at war, of the East or of the West, Christian or Islamic, are, in various forms and in different degrees, now worshiping.

---

[97] Britannica

Their high priests are the politicians and the worldly-wise, the so-called sages of the age; their sacrifice, the flesh and blood of the slaughtered multitudes; their incantations outworn shibboleths and insidious and irreverent formulas; their incense, the smoke of anguish that ascends from the lacerated hearts of the bereaved, the maimed, and the homeless.[98]

Bahá'u'lláh's letters to kings and rulers, written while confined in Adrianople, foretold the difficulties of the future. Of the recipients, Save for England, whose Queen, Victoria, responded with kindness, their kingdoms and dynasty became extinct. Wrath and a storm of change continue on into the beginning of the 21st-Century. His letters are contained in the *Proclamation of Bahá'u'lláh.*[99] Initial demise of the old order is discussed in the *Promised Day Has Come.*[100]

As humanity initiates the new Century and Millennium, it has become manifestly clear that interdependence of nations demands cooperation. Nations are turning toward the concept of collective security and the need for International Law as expressed by the United Nations. Pivotal to the resolution of these problems is the matter of racial differences, or the need for recognition of the oneness of mankind. Prejudices are widespread but progress is being made.

And every island fled away, and the mountains were not found. And there fell upon men a great hail out of heaven, every stone about the weight of a talent: and men blasphemed God because of the plague of the hail; for the plague thereof was exceeding great. (20-21)

Islands sanctuaries and mountainous institutions of the past were not found. Great heavenly instructions provided a new inheritance but, because of the difficulty for obedience to them, were to some of humanity a torment likened to a plague of hail.

---

[98] Shoghi Effendi, *The Promised Day is Come,* Bahá'í Publishing Trust, Wilmette, Illinois, p. 117.
[99] Baha'u'llah, *Proclamation of Baha'u'llah,* Baha'i World Center, Haifa, Israel.
[100] Shoghi Effendi, *Promised Day is Come,* Bahá'í Publishing Trust, Wilmette, Illinois.

Old Social Order

Chapters 17 and 18

Immediately after the tribulation of those days shall the sun be darkened, and the moon shall not give her light, and the stars shall fall from heaven, and the powers of the heavens shall be shaken: And then shall appear the sign of the Son of man in heaven: and then shall all the tribes of the earth mourn, and they shall see the Son of man coming in the clouds of heaven with power and great glory. And he shall send his angels with a great sound of a trumpet, and they shall gather together his elect from the four winds, from one end of heaven to the other.

Mat 24:29-31

Revelation Chapter 17

The Mystery

And there came one of the seven angels which had the seven vials, and talked with me, saying unto me, Come hither; I will show unto thee the judgment of the great whore that sitteth upon many waters: With whom the kings of the earth have committed fornication, and the inhabitants of the earth have been made drunk with the wine of her fornication. So he carried me away in the spirit into the wilderness: and I saw a woman sit upon a scarlet coloured beast, full of names of blasphemy, having seven heads and ten horns. (1-3)

The message of the Book of Revelation to all the peoples of the world, symbolized by its immediate recipients, the seven religions of Chapters 2 and 3, continues as John hears one of the seven angels who had had one of the vials of wrath. Discussion repeats, in a modified form, some material of Chapters 12 and 13 concerning conditions of Islam under the Umayyads. *"I will show unto thee the judgment of the great whore... the inhabitants of the earth have been made drunk with the wine of her fornication."* The kings of the earth, by corrupting the intent of Muhammad's teachings, have misguided nations of Islam.

John was carried away in the spirit to see the mystery of the woman and the beast. The woman, signalizing the great city, sat upon the *"scarlet colored beast"* of the Umayyads. Seven heads represent the seven domains or administrative centers of that dynasty (12:3, p. 122). The ten horns symbolize the names of successive kings, and scarlet portrays a color of religion.

And the woman was arrayed in purple and scarlet colour, and decked with gold and precious stones and pearls, having a golden cup in her hand full of abominations and filthiness of her fornication: And upon her forehead was a name written, MYSTERY, BABYLON THE GREAT, THE MOTHER OF HARLOTS AND ABOMINATIONS OF THE EARTH. And I saw the woman drunken with the blood of the saints, and with the blood of the martyrs of Jesus: and when I saw her, I wondered with great admiration. (4-6)

The woman, in her compromised state, represents the applied Law of God under the denigrating influence of the beast and dragon. Although arrayed in purple, scarlet, gold, and precious stones—the symbolic apparel of religious authority—she was under control of followers of the beast. She had become the mother of deprecated morality and drunken with the blood of persecuted saints. Her temperament resulted from the dragon that represented the full dynastic reign of the Umayyads and the persecution of rightful heirs of Muhammad.

The name of the dissolute Holy City is BABYLON. She was the "MOTHER OF HARLOTS," the successive kingdoms of the dynasty.

And the angel said unto me, Wherefore didst thou marvel? I will tell thee the mystery of the woman, and of the beast that carrieth her, which hath the seven heads and ten horns. The beast that thou sawest was, and is not; and shall ascend out of the bottomless pit, and go into perdition: and they that dwell on the earth shall wonder, whose names were not written in the book of life from the foundation of the world, when they behold the beast that was, and is not, and yet is. And here is the mind which hath wisdom. The seven heads are seven mountains, on which the woman sitteth. (7-9)

One of the seven angels of the vials, an angel of the new order, offered to explain to John the mystery of the woman and of the beast with seven heads and ten horns who carried her. The beast is from out of the bottomless pit, Chapter 9, and was introduced by verse 11:7. The beast is the Umayyad Dynasty whose reign was initiated by Mu'áwíyah. As instigator of this dynastic reign, Mu'áwíyah is a paradigm of beastly qualities.

Mu'áwíyah, Governor of Syria, assumed upon Alí's death Power of State without having legal authority. This action weakened his own base of support because it lacked followers of Medina who were true to Muhammad and His posterity. In an attempt to strengthen his position, Mu'áwíyah negotiated with Alí's eldest son, Hasan, for the legal position of Caliph; Hasan was rightful heir in the hereditary line of Muhammad and should have been second Imam but was obliged to complete this negotiation. Hasan was in a weakened position because of events relating to his father, Alí's death, and had little control of Mu'áwíyah. Hasan turned powers of state over to

Mu'áwíyah with the proviso that leadership, upon Mu'áwíyah death,[101] would return to rightful heirs.

From this sequence of events, Mu'áwíyah, *was* self appointed Caliph following the death of Alí but acknowledged Hasan as rightful heir, therefore *is not* and following the agreement with Hasan became Caliph, *yet is.* Mu'áwíyah followers should wonder at his success!

The above interpretation and that of the following riddle are explained in reference to the kings and leaders of the Umayyads, which are known as the beast. The riddles have also been explained in relation to similarities between the territories of the Persian Empire under Cyrus the Great, the Greek Empire under Alexander the Great, and Islam under the Umayyads.[102]

There were seven geographical regions, which supported the kings, v. 12:3, p. 120, of the Umayyad dynasty. Each domain as part of a theocracy in concert with its kings and heads of state represented a mountain of authority in comparison to ordinary organization. Usurping and destroying the application of Islamic spiritual power, the condition of state, under the tutelage of the Umayyads, became the woman whose name was Babylon.

And there are seven kings: five are fallen, and one is, and the other is not yet come; and when he cometh, he must continue a short space. And the beast that was, and is not, even he is the eighth, and is of the seven, and goeth into perdition. (10-11)

The riddle refers to the beast in respect to its champions and can be explained by review of leaders that resulted in the take over of power by the Umayyads, as follows: Five kings are fallen. These were—Abu Sufyan, Amir of Mecca and chief of the dynasty of the Umayyads,[103] Abu-Bakr, 'Umar, 'Uthman, and Alí, *five.* That is, the chief of the Umayyad Dynasty, the first three Caliphs, and Alí the fourth Caliph and first Imam, making *five.* Following these, one is, Mu'áwíyah, *six.* He was the Governor of Syria and had

---

[101] H. M. Balyuzi, *Muhammad and the Course of Islam,* George Ronald, Oxford p. 187.
[102] Robert F. Riggs, *The Apocalypse Revealed,* Philosophical Library, New York, Chapter 13.
[103] 'Abdu'l-Bahá, *Some Answered Questions,* Bahá'í Publishing Trust, Wilmette, Illinois, p. 69.

never accepted Alí as the fourth Caliph. A power struggle ensued and some fanatics killed Alí. By default, Mu'áwíyah became the *sixth* king.

Alí 's eldest son, Hasan, was the rightful heir. He represents, in the riddle, one who is to come for a short space. Hasan's military support was weak because of the troubles between Mu'áwíyah and Alí. Hasan had no real choice other than to make an agreement with Mu'áwíyah to abdicate.[104] The agreement recognizes Hasan's abdication so that for a time Hasan was, in effect, Caliph and Imam, *seven*.

After Hasan's abdication, Mu'áwíyah was again Caliph, *eight,* and fulfilled—*"was, is not, even he is the eighth, and is of the seven."* He was also of the *seven* because of assuming authority upon Alí 's death. Mu'áwíyah was the beast and this agrees with the explanations of Chapter 12 and 13.

This riddle can also be explained in relation to continuation of the seven territories of early Islam.[105] With this alternative explanation, the second beast becomes the 'Abbásid Dynasty.

These events mark continuance of the division between the Shí'ah Imamate and the Sunní Caliphate that are the two major sects of Islam. Alí was the fourth Caliph and the first Imam. Caliphs are *elected* and leaned toward the political while the Imams hold *hereditary* office and a spiritual position.

And the ten horns which thou sawest are ten kings, which have received no kingdom as yet; but receive power as kings one hour with the beast. These have one mind, and shall give their power and strength unto the beast. (12-13)

The fourteen kings of the Umayyads and Abu Sufyan, Chief of the Umayyad Dynasty, had ten names (horns) during a hundred fourteen year rule. Each king ruled for an *"hour,"* and with one mind gave power unto the great red dragon and to the Islamic territories. Their average tenure of office was about 1/24 of a day, or year, and likened to an hour of prophetic time.[106]

---

[104] H.M. Balyuzi, *Muhammad and the Course of Islam*, George Ronald, Oxford, p. 187.
[105] Robert F. Riggs, *The Apocalypse Unsealed,* Philosophical Library, New York, Chapter 17.
[106] Ibid, p. 210.

These shall make war with the Lamb, and the Lamb shall overcome them: for he is Lord of lords, and King of kings: and they that are with him are called, and chosen, and faithful. And he saith unto me, The waters which thou sawest, where the whore sitteth, are peoples, and multitudes, and nations, and tongues. (14-15)

At the end of the Islamic Dispensation, dragon-like qualities of the whore that make war with the Lamb will be conquered by God's Cause, that is, renewed by Bahá'u'lláh and His followers. Conquest progresses by expansion and growth of the new religion. Those who participate are *"called and chosen,"* Chapter 14.

Waters where the whore sitteth represent the *"peoples, and multitudes, and nations, and tongues"* of the seven domains.

And the ten horns which thou sawest upon the beast, these shall hate the whore, and shall make her desolate and naked, and shall eat her flesh, and burn her with fire.(16)

The ten horns (names of individual leaders) *"shall eat her flesh"* and make her desolate. The Umayyads were enemies of Muhammad and the Islamic Faith. They caused His message to become as a "dead body" in the street, v. 11:8, p. 109. Without the original spirit of the Law of God, its administration becomes known as a "whore."

For God hath put in their hearts to fulfil his will, and to agree, and give their kingdom unto the beast, until the words of God shall be fulfilled. (17)

The will of God transcends the affairs of men. The prophecy of the Book of Revelation shall be fulfilled; the Umayyads and the Islamic dispensation played their part in a foreordained historic role.

And the woman which thou sawest is that great city, which reigneth over the kings of the earth. (18)

The great city is that Holy City, Jerusalem, which is sometimes signified as a Woman that normally reflects the Law of God. When administration of the Religion of God becomes corrupted, the Holy City is known as Babylon or whore. It takes on the form of the outer court of verse 11:1, p. 105. (Also 16:19, p. 161.)

Revelation Chapter 18

Old Order Falls

And after these things I saw another angel come down from heaven, having great power; and the earth was lightened with his glory. And he cried mightily with a strong voice, saying, Babylon the great is fallen, is fallen, and is become the habitation of devils, and the hold of every foul spirit, and a cage of every unclean and hateful bird. For all nations have drunk of the wine of the wrath of her fornication, and the kings of the earth have committed fornication with her, and the merchants of the earth are waxed rich through the abundance of her delicacies. (1-3)

The Angel of renewal cries out, *"Babylon the great is fallen"* and also comments on Babylon's dispirited character. Kings have compromised their kingdoms and *"merchants of the earth"* are made rich because of the abundance of her resources.

The three dimensional flight of birds in their natural habitat represent man's free spirit, a condition which can be contrasted with the legacy of the bottomless pit of error that made *"unclean and hateful birds"* of men's hearts. The present world condition generally entertains similar qualities. People of the world, caged by the dragon of evil, and suffering great difficulties seem entrapped in a continuing condition of world chaos.

Worldly desires, the prime mover of modern commerce, have made nations, kings and merchants rich. In the new millennium, this condition represents near universal suppression of spiritual values and the wholehearted acceptance of materialism.

Come Out Of Her

And I heard another voice from heaven, saying, Come out of her, my people, that ye be not partakers of her sins, and that ye receive not of her plagues. For her sins have reached unto heaven, and God hath remembered her iniquities. Reward her even as she rewarded you, and double unto her double according to her works: in the cup which she hath filled fill to her double. How much she hath glorified herself, and lived deliciously, so much torment and sorrow give her: for she saith in her heart, I sit a queen, and am no widow, and shall see no sorrow.

Therefore shall her plagues come in one day, death, and mourning, and famine; and she shall
be utterly burned with fire: for strong is the Lord God who judgeth her. (4-8)

Those who refuse the Word of God at the time of religious renewal and
remain with the old order, partake of her past sins. With each new religious
dispensation, the Prophet, His disciples, and all others working for social rebirth, urge the people to remove themselves from the past and enter the
paradise of spiritual renewal appropriate to a new age. Specifically, the Bahá'í
message was first addressed to the Muslims and people of Persia. Within
about a century, the message of Bahá'u'lláh was made available to the whole
world.

Abdu'l-Bahá, the eldest son of Bahá'u'lláh and servant of the Glory, was
an indispensable support throughout His Father's ministry and forty year
banishment. Following this, His service was extended for the twenty-nine
year period of His own ministry. With power and wisdom inherent to a
unique station and unknown to the course of past religions, he guided many
in their search after religious truth. Shoghi Effendi comments on the qualities
of 'Abdu'l-Bahá:

> I am not sure whether I have sent you before a copy of this glorious
> Tablet revealed by Bahá'u'lláh for His beloved Abdu'l-Bahá, written
> in His own blessed handwriting, and which we found among his pa-
> pers and documents soon after the Master's Ascension [physical
> death and spiritual continuation]. It reveals in terms of touching ten-
> derness the unique station of Abdu'l-Bahá, and constitutes an un-
> challengeable evidence of His supreme authority. [107]

In the following two passages 'Abdu'l-Bahá pleads with the people of Persia, home of the Bahá'í revelation. He points out their present predicament
and asks them to relinquish their inactivity combined with a false sense of
worth:

> Were not the people of Persia, in days long gone, the head and
> front of intellect and wisdom? Did they not, by God's grace, shine

---

[107] Shoghi Effendi, *Bahá'í Administration,* Bahá'í Publishing Trust, Wilmette, Illinois, p. 48.

out like the daystar from the horizons of Divine knowledge? How is it that we are satisfied today with this miserable condition, are engrossed in our licentious passions, have blinded ourselves to supreme happiness, to that which is pleasing in God's sight, and have all become absorbed in our selfish concerns and the search for ignoble, personal advantage? [108]

O people of Persia! How long will your torpor and lethargy last? … You who once lit the world, how is it that you lurk, inert, bemused, in darkness now? Open your mind's eye, see your great and present need. Rise up and struggle, seek education, seek enlightenment. … Is it commendable that you should waste and fritter away in apathy the brilliance that is your birthright, your native competence, your inborn understanding?[109]

The function of revelation is to create spiritual change, and in this respect, the Old Order will pass away as people become obedient to the renewed Law of God and remove themselves from Babylon's control. This process represents the resurrection function of religion. Although the general content of the Book of Revelation in its development of a renewal paradigm centers on Islam's experience, implications of the period of the third woe point to similar experiences throughout the world. Beyond Islam and the Umayyad paradigm of error, present day difficulties are recognized by Bahá'í teachings as being worldwide in scope. Accordingly, 'Abdu'l-Bahá, while visiting in America, made his plea for the people to join in the effort of working toward the new heaven of spirit and new earth of thought.

I have come here with this mission: that through your endeavors, through your heavenly morals, through your devoted efforts a perfect bond of unity and love may be established between the East and the West so that the bestowals of God may descend upon all and that all may be seen to be the parts of the same tree - the great tree of the human family. For mankind may be likened to the

---

[108] 'Abdu'l-Bahá, *Secret of Divine Civilization,* Bahá'í Publishing Trust, Wilmette, Illinois, p. 9
[109] Ibid, p. 91-92

branches, leaves, blossoms and fruit of that tree.[110] (See also p. 143.)

The need for a multitude of new followers, who recognize religious renewal, that is, to "overcome," was anticipated in Chapter 2 and 3. This requirement is a central issue of The Book of Revelation and, by way of explanation, places emphasis on Babylon's lack of spiritual qualities. In regard to mankind's purpose, Bahá'u'lláh has stated:

> All men have been created to carry forward an ever-advancing civilization. The Almighty beareth Me witness: To act like the beasts of the field is unworthy of man.[111]

Babylon, allowed to drink from her own cup of wickedness, will fall. Negative qualities, relentless conditions of wickedness as witnessed by assessment of today's social environment, cannot sustain a viable way of planetary existence.

Debased because of beastly traits within her territories, the noble origin of Babylon is elusive and forgotten even to the extent of her own unawareness that she no longer professes human virtues, i.e., that the quality of religion, as practiced, is no longer symbolized by the marriage of the Bridegroom, the Word of God, to the Holy City or Material Law of God.

Confronted with the purging influence of the returned Word of God, and finding its message contrary to her desires, she must suffer from plague and censure. This period of time, one day of the Lord, may be a religious dispensation; nevertheless, dramatic world conditions will bring rapid changes. The judgment will be sudden, possibly a few decades at its climax. However, the healing period brought by the Word of God ordinarily extends over a period of centuries.

Kings of the Earth Shall Bewail Her

And the kings of the earth, who have committed fornication and lived deliciously with her, shall bewail her, and lament for her, when they shall see the smoke of her burning, (9)

---

[110] 'Abdu'l-Bahá, *Promulgation of Universal Peace,* Bahá'í Publishing Trust, Wilmette, Illinois, p. 13.
[111] Bahá'u'lláh, *Gleanings from the Writings of Bahá'u'lláh,* Bahá'í Publishing Trust, Wilmette, Illinois p. 215.

Vested interests, caught in smoldering change, shall forfeit their power and wail over lost alliances of political, economic, and religious relationships, and become lost in the *"smoke of her burning."*

Standing afar off for the fear of her torment, saying, Alas, alas that great city Babylon, that mighty city! for in one hour is thy judgment come. And the merchants of the earth shall weep and mourn over her, for no man buyeth their merchandise any more: The merchandise of gold, and silver, and precious stones, and of pearls, and fine linen, and purple, and silk, and scarlet, and all thyine wood, and all manner vessels of ivory, and all manner vessels of most precious wood, and of brass, and iron, and marble, And cinnamon, and odours, and ointments, and frankincense, and wine, and oil, and fine flour, and wheat, and beasts, and sheep, and horses, and chariots, and slaves, and souls of men. (10-13)

Merchants of the earth shall weep and mourn because commercial practices, as previously experienced, will cease to exist. With destruction of *"that great city Babylon"* humanity will simultaneously attain to a new level of morality and incorporate elements of world unity and peace. When spiritual maturity transcends attachment to materialism, an awakening to the value of the souls of men will become apparent.

And the fruits that thy soul lusted after are departed from thee, and all things which were dainty and goodly are departed from thee, and thou shalt find them no more at all. (14)

Forbidden fruit of past experience, including frivolous material things, are gone from Babylon. Newly found spiritual values will lead to significant social change.

The merchants of these things, which were made rich by her, shall stand afar off for the fear of her torment, weeping and wailing, And saying, Alas, alas, that great city, that was clothed in fine linen, and purple, and scarlet, and decked with gold, and precious stones, and pearls! For in one hour so great riches is come to nought. And every shipmaster, and all the company in ships, and sailors, and as many as trade by sea, stood afar off, And cried when they saw the smoke of her burning, saying, What city is like unto this great city! And they cast dust on their heads, and cried, weeping and wailing, saying, Alas, alas, that great city, wherein were made rich all that had ships in the sea by reason of her costliness! for in one hour is she made desolate. (15-19)

All observers shall be surprised at the change in fortune of *"that great city,"* the Law of God. Babylon came clothed *"in fine linen"* and other items of decor all confirming her religious credentials, but misrepresentation of her spiritual purpose led to her demise. Love of materialism became the bane of existence and compromised spiritual values through out the entire world.

Those who trade in the sea of religious and commercial beliefs, leaders of all types, *"cried when they saw the smoke of her burning."* They shall cry over the demise of past organization and wonder what can possibly replace the Babylonian arrangements of the past—*"what city is like unto this great city!"*

New approaches were a costly loss to those of past enterprises; their ships in the sea of social depravity and materialism, manifesting deception and lust, were of no value.

The Faithful Can Rejoice

Rejoice over her, thou heaven, and ye holy apostles and prophets; for God hath avenged you on her. And a mighty angel took up a stone like a great millstone, and cast it into the sea, saying, Thus with violence shall that great city Babylon be thrown down, and shall be found no more at all. And the voice of harpers, and musicians, and of pipers, and trumpeters, shall be heard no more at all in thee; and no craftsman, of whatsoever craft he be, shall be found any more in thee; and the sound of a millstone shall be heard no more at all in thee; And the light of a candle shall shine no more at all in thee; and the voice of the bridegroom and of the bride shall be heard no more at all in thee: for thy merchants were the great men of the earth; for by thy sorceries were all nations deceived. And in her was found the blood of prophets, and of saints, and of all that were slain upon the earth. (20-24)

Those who work for the cause of God as the 21st-Century begins should rejoice because a new order of world enterprise and unity is developing; organization reflecting spiritual understanding is forming the foundation of a new creation. During the transition sudden and difficult disturbances arise. Social destruction is approaching climactic proportions, and dramatic interruptions occur everyday. This century has been one of near continuous warfare, and the end of violence is presently unknown. Positive qualities of the old order have atrophied; human virtues have largely disappeared in social transactions. The true spirit of the Religion of God is no longer found in the practice of the Holy City, but the renewed Law of God, married to a new order, shall be reinstated.

The origin of the woman, a product of Muhammad's revelation, who became Babylon, was noble, and many of her prophets and saints in the past have worked and suffered for the Cause of God. Each dispensation begins with the ideals of new revelation and suffers persecution by the powers of the old order.

"And in her was found the blood of prophets, and of saints."

New Social Order
Chapters 19-22

This is the Day whereon naught can be seen except the splendors of the Light that shineth from the face of Thy Lord, the Gracious, the Most Bountiful. Verily, We have caused every soul to expire by virtue of Our irresistible and all-subduing sovereignty. We have, then, called into being a new creation, as a token of Our grace unto men. I am, verily, the All-Bountiful, the Ancient of Days. This is the Day whereon the unseen world crieth out: "Great is thy blessedness, O earth, for thou hast been made the foot-stool of thy God, and been chosen as the seat of His mighty throne." The realm of glory exclaimeth: "Would that my life could be sacrificed for thee, for He Who is the Beloved of the All-Merciful hath established His sovereignty upon thee, through the power of His Name that hath been promised unto all things, whether of the past or of the future."

Gleanings, pp 29-30

Revelation Chapter 19

The Bridegroom

And after these things I heard a great voice of much people e in heaven, saying, Alleluia; Salvation, and glory, and honour, and power, unto the Lord our God: For true and righteous are his judgments: for he hath judged the great whore, which did corrupt the earth with her fornication, and hath avenged the blood of his servants at her hand. And again they said, Alleluia. And her smoke rose up for ever and ever. (1-3)

John's attention shifted as he heard a multitude of voices that had accepted spiritual renewal from the Word of God for this age. They praised God for renewing His Laws; He has judged the status quo of a disconnected world, *"and hath avenged the blood of his servants"* that suffered at the hands of past leaders. The blindness of evil likened unto smoke from the fire of destruction rose up forever and ever.

And the four and twenty elders and the four beasts fell down and worshipped God that sat on the throne, saying, Amen; Alleluia. And a voice came out of the throne, saying, Praise our God, all ye his servants, and ye that fear him, both small and great. (4-5)

The twenty-four elders and four beasts, introduced in Chapter 4 as faithful servants of God's renewed Cause, fell down and worshipped *"God that sat on the throne."* Eighteen of the elders were disciples of the Báb. They and the Báb were all martyred. Their tragic story is told in the *Dawn-Breakers*.[112] The remaining elders and the four friendly beasts have not as yet been specified because fulfillment continues to unfold in our time. Their identity will be recognized in the future. (p. 60)

The Prophet, in representing God, speaks for Him and figuratively sits on a throne. It is the voice of the Prophet that can be heard. And this we

---

[112] Nabíl, *The Dawn-Breakers,* Bahá'í Publishing Trust, Wilmette, Illinois, various Chapters.

conclude would be Bahá'u'lláh Who comes as the Father and Lord of Hosts. He is saying, *"Praise our God."* He is God's Prophet, Agent, or Manifestation, but the Prophet is not to be confused with the Essence of God. God is made known through His Prophets that are separate from God. In spiritual authority, they are God so far as humanity is concerned.[113]

The Voice of Servants

And I heard as it were the voice of a great multitude, and as the voice of many waters, and as the voice of mighty thunderings, saying, Alleluia: for the Lord God omnipotent reigneth. (6)

The voice of numerous followers from the new revelation could be heard as a great multitude. Proclamation is the first phase of revelation and is likened to praise combined with thunderings. The multitudes were as a voice of many spiritual waters because, although coming from diverse cultural roots and native religions, they acknowledge the oneness of the Spirit. The oneness of God, His Prophets, and His Religions constitute a central teaching of the Bahá'í Faith.

Let us be glad and rejoice, and give honour to him: for the marriage of the Lamb is come, and his wife hath made herself ready. And to her was granted that she should be arrayed in fine linen, clean and white: for the fine linen is the righteousness of saints.(7-8)

All those aligned with the Spirit of this age should rejoice and honor God for He has sent His Prophet, as Lamb, to rejuvenate the Law of God that is metaphorically the wife of the Prophet. The Law of God is *"arrayed in fine linen, clean and white: for the fine linen is the righteousness of saints."* The Law of God for this age displays its credentials because of those who work for its expression in human affairs. Through them, the mission of the Prophet in setting forth the Law of God becomes a reality, and this effort is the theme of the times.

---

[113] Bahá'u'lláh, *Gleanings from the Writings of Bahá'u'lláh,* Bahá'í Publishing Trust, Wilmette, Illinois. p. 66.

The Marriage Supper

And he saith unto me, Write, Blessed are they which are called unto the marriage supper of the Lamb. And he saith unto me, These are the true sayings of God. And I fell at his feet to worship him. And he said unto me, See thou do it not: I am thy fellowservant, and of thy brethren that have the testimony of Jesus: worship God: for the testimony of Jesus is the spirit of prophecy. (9-10)

Blessed are they in the spirit of the Lamb and His marriage; they are called to the marriage supper. Without knowledge of His teachings, how can one see the importance of spiritual renewal and be aware of the pending marriage of the Lamb?

The Speaker claims His authority with a declaration: *"These are the true sayings of God."* Nevertheless, He tells John not to fall at His feet while at the same time reminding him that He speaks for God as testified by Jesus Who is the spirit of prophecy: The Prophet is a *"fellowservant"* and gives a command to worship God as noted above and also in Verses 1:17, p. 50; 19:4-5, p. 181; and 22:8-9, p. 209.

> Thus it is that the accents of God Himself have been heard uttered by these Manifestations of the divine Being.
>
> Viewed in the light of their second station - the station of distinction, differentiation, temporal limitations, characteristics and standards, - they manifest absolute servitude, utter destitution and complete self-effacement. Even as He saith: 'I am the servant of God. I am but a man like you.'[114]

And I saw heaven opened, and behold a white horse; and he that sat upon him was called Faithful and True, and in righteousness he doth judge and make war. His eyes were as a flame of fire, and on his head were many crowns; and he had a name written, that no man knew, but he himself. And he was clothed with a vesture dipped in blood: and his name is called The Word of God. (11-13)

---

[114] Baha'u'llah, *Kitáb-i-Íqán,* , Baha'i Publishing Trust, Wilmette, Illinois, p. 178.

John sees in the heaven of spiritual vision a description of the Bride-groom: He rides the *"white horse"* of spiritual power and does *"judge and make war"* with those who have severed themselves from His Message. He is the Word of God and wears many crowns because of numerous revelations and because Prophets have at various times championed God's Cause. Numerous persecutions have dipped His vesture in blood. Nevertheless, in each age He renews the Law of God, that Holy City, the bride of the Lamb, also known as New Jerusalem.

And the armies which were in heaven followed him upon white horses, clothed in fine linen, white and clean. And out of his mouth goeth a sharp sword, that with it he should smite the nations: and he shall rule them with a rod of iron: and he treadeth the winepress of the fierceness and wrath of Almighty God. (14-15)

Armies living in the heaven of belief follow the Prophet and Lord of Hosts. With the *"sharp sword"* of the Word of God He shall *"smite the nations"* and *"shall rule them with a rod of iron."* His teachings break traditions and through pressure of *"fierceness and wrath"* bring the pattern for a unified world, v. 14:17-20, p. 143.

And he hath on his vesture and on his thigh a name written, KING OF KINGS, AND LORD OF LORDS. (16)

Bahá'u'lláh comes as the Father and is therefore the KING OF KINGS, AND LORD OF LORDS. He is the supreme Manifestation of the Bahá'í Cycle that began with Adam's command.

> The Bahá'í cycle is, indeed, incomparable in its greatness. It includes not only the Prophets that will appear after Bahá'u'lláh, but all those who have preceded Him ever since Adam. These should, indeed, be viewed as constituting but preliminary stages

leading gradually to the appearance of this supreme Manifestation of God. [115]

And I saw an angel standing in the sun; and he cried with a loud voice, saying to all the fowls that fly in the midst of heaven, Come and gather yourselves together unto the supper of the great God; That ye may eat the flesh of kings, and the flesh of captains, and the flesh of mighty men, and the flesh of horses, and of them that sit on them, and the flesh of all men, both free and bond, both small and great. (17-18)

An angel standing in the source of spiritual reality, symbolized as the sun and experienced as new teachings, calls followers of new revelation into action. Immediate progress is with the supper of God: that is, learning the Word of God for this age and participating in its teaching.

Only the followers of the Lamb, those who are aware of spiritual renewal, are called to the *"marriage supper"*. The supper becomes a celebration in preparation for the union of the Prophet, the Word of God, and His bride known as the Holy City, or material Law of God. The process of religious renewal resurrects the human spirit in order to carry forward the advancement of civilization.

The fowls of heaven, unclean and hateful birds of men's hearts, can destroy (eat the flesh) the life and power of the beast and his cohorts—kings, captains, mighty men, horses, their riders, all men, free, bond, small and great. These verses anticipate final conquest of the Old Order.

The Kings of the Earth

And I saw the beast, and the kings of the earth, and their armies, gathered together to make war against him that sat on the horse, and against his army. And the beast was taken, and with him the false prophet that wrought miracles before him, with which he deceived them that had received the mark of the beast, and them that worshipped his image. These both were cast alive into a lake of fire burning with brimstone. And the remnant were slain with the sword of him that sat upon the horse, which sword proceeded out of his mouth: and all the fowls were filled with their flesh. (19-21)

---

[115] Shoghi Effendi, *Directives of the Guardian,* Bahá'í Publishing Trust, New Delhi, pp. 7-8.

The beast and kings from out of the bottomless pit *"were cast alive into a lake of fire burning with brimstone."* From the burning condemnation of error, transformation shall continue until the Law of God subdues the beast and false prophets. Withering of beastly qualities continues as progress toward world unity advances.

Thus, the remnant were slain (conquered) by the Word of God and the supper was ended.

Revelation Chapter 20

Binding the Dragon

And I saw an angel come down from heaven, having the key of the bottomless pit and a great chain in his hand. And he laid hold on the dragon, that old serpent, which is the Devil, and Satan, and bound him a thousand years, (1-2)

An angel with *"the key of the bottomless pit"* is able through revelation to chain up for one full dispensation, or the millennium, the circulation of ignorance from the bottomless pit of error. These characteristics, both devastating and bottomless in their scope, are the root cause of *"the dragon, that old serpent, which is the Devil and Satan,"* and must in each renewal of religion yield to the reinstated Law of God. Bahá'u'lláh, in celebration of the return of Jesus Christ, brings enlightenment, the key that opens the door to spiritual understanding.

And cast him into the bottomless pit, and shut him up, and set a seal upon him, that he should deceive the nations no more, till the thousand years should be fulfilled: and after that he must be loosed a little season. (3)

Teachings of this age, uniquely for a global civilization, will cast international anarchy appearing as attributes of the dragon generated from ignorance into the bottomless pit and inspire development of world unity. Humanity's stymied progress for eons has been replete with the problem of warring peoples and dysfunctional centers of power. Nations of the future will be at peace until "the end days" of the thousand years when Satan is *"loosed a little season"* and another correction is required.

Renewed Authority

And I saw thrones, and they sat upon them, and judgment was given unto them: and I saw the souls of them that were beheaded for the witness of Jesus, and for the word of

God, and which had not worshipped the beast, neither his image, neither had received his mark upon their foreheads, or in their hands; and they lived and reigned with Christ a thousand years. (4)

Clergy of the past have sat on the throne of judgment and authority. Now members of Faith, spiritually and administrative united, without benefit of clergy, shall perform this function. The renewed system working within a modified form of democracy shall be subservient to the Law of God as revealed for this age by Bahá'u'lláh. Clearly, all martyrs for the cause of God are physically dead but spiritually alive. They *"lived and reigned with Christ a thousand years"* in the heavenly realm, while those on earth, who do not succumb to the beast, live their life in a heavenly surrounding that acknowledges the Spirit of God.

First Resurrection

But the rest of the dead lived not again until the thousand years were finished. This is the first resurrection. Blessed and holy is he that hath part in the first resurrection: on such the second death hath no power, but they shall be priests of God and of Christ, and shall reign with him a thousand years. (5-6)

"Blessed and holy is he that hath part in the first resurrection." Persons who avoid the *"first [spiritual] resurrection"* offered by Bahá'u'lláh's teachings must wait until the next revelation in order to have another opportunity when the process begins anew.

> Behold how the generality of mankind hath been endued with the capacity to hearken unto God's most exalted Word—the Word upon which must depend the gathering together and spiritual resurrection of all men....[116]

"The resurrected" of this revelation shall participate in God's Cause in the heavenly realm of spiritual renewal and shall be the earthly *"priests"* of God and of the Spirit of Christ. They *"shall reign with him a thousand years."*

---

[116] Bahá'u'lláh, *Gleanings from the Writings of Bahá'u'lláh,* Bahá'í Publishing Trust, Wilmette, Illinois, p. 97.

They who do not respond to the resurrection of this Day, not "born again," suffer the second death. Similarly, those who missed the Revelation of Jesus Christ suffered the first death.[117]

Recurring Last Days

And when the thousand years are expired, Satan shall be loosed out of his prison, And shall go out to deceive the nations which are in the four quarters of the earth, Gog and Magog, to gather them together to battle: the number of whom is as the sand of the sea. (7-8)

The true spirit of renewal dissipates over centuries of time; then, *"Satan shall be loosed"* and create disruptive conditions associated with "last days." Then another revelation is required to resurrect the Word of God. Although the future world structure is uncertain at present, verses imply that, in the age of world unity, there may be a modified arrangement of nations which makes them as numerous *"as the sand of the sea."*

> After Bahá'u'lláh many Prophets will, no doubt, appear but they will be under His Shadow. Although they may abrogate the laws of this Dispensation in accordance with the needs and requirements of the age in which they appear, they nevertheless draw their spiritual force from this mighty Revelation. The Faith of Bahá'u'lláh constitutes, indeed, the stage of maturity in the development of mankind. His appearance has released such spiritual forces which will continue to animate, for many long years to come, the world in its development. Whatever progress may be achieved, in later ages, after the unification of the whole human race is achieved, will be but improvement in the machinery of the world. For the machinery itself has been already created by Bahá'u'lláh. The task of continually improving and perfecting this machinery is one which later Prophets will be called upon to achieve. They will thus move and work within the orbit of the Baha'i Cycle.[118]

---

[117] Robert F. Riggs, *The Apocalypse Unsealed,* Philosophical Library, New York, p. 227.
[118] Shoghi Effendi, *Directives of the Guardian,* Bahá'í Publishing Trust, New Delhi, pp. 61-62.

Saved by Renewal

And they went up on the breadth of the earth, and compassed the camp of the saints about, and the beloved city: and fire came down from God out of heaven, and devoured them. (9)

At the end of the dispensation of Bahá'u'lláh, in its last days when the enemies of faith have surrounded the camp of the saints, *"fire"* of the Word will once more destroy the endeavor of the ignorant. Renewal of the beloved city, which is the Holy City, Jerusalem, or Law of God, shall become a reality. The outer court, vv. 11:1-2, p. 105, of spiritual depravation, encompassing the entire globe of that time, will again be renewed.

And the devil that deceived them was cast into the lake of fire and brimstone, where the beast and the false prophet are, and shall be tormented day and night for ever and ever. (10)

The *"devil [of ignorance] that deceived them"* was cast back into the realm of the uninspired in which the substance of the *"beast and false prophet"* resides. Problems of the *human spirit* must once more be sorted out. But in a future world, organized on the basis of world unity, the next corrective action may last *"for ever and ever."*

And I saw a great white throne, and him that sat on it, from whose face the earth and the heaven fled away; and there was found no place for them. (11)

The Seat of the Universal House of Justice, built from marble, is situated in the midst of the Bahá'í Gardens that are located on Mount Carmel in Haifa, Israel. Members of this Supreme Executive and Spiritual Body of the Bahá'í World are responsible to the laws of Bahá'u'lláh. With reinstatement of this *"great white throne"* of Authority within the worldwide community of the "last days" of the Bahá'í dispensation, *"there was found no place for"* a misrepresented earth and heaven. God's authority shall be visible and unified because of mankind's singleness of purpose under the Law of God.

And I saw the dead, small and great, stand before God; and the books were opened: and another book was opened, which is the book of life: and the dead were judged out of those things which were written in the books, according to their works. (12)

All *"the dead, small and great"* existing under the protection of the books of God and living at a standard of conduct as recorded in the *"book of life"* had been judged in reference to these works.

And the sea gave up the dead which were in it; and death and hell delivered up the dead which were in them: and they were judged every man according to their works. (13)

Every man, for *"the sea [of humanity] gave up the dead which were in it,"* shall be judged according to the extent of his understanding and works. Works in this context implies faith in God, obedience to His Laws, and endeavor for improvement of self and community. Renewal and social revision for the needs of that age shall guide people of spiritual maturity. It is an age of general understanding in which *"the books were opened"* and of highest expectations.

And death and hell were cast into the lake of fire. This is the second death. And whosoever was not found written in the book of life was cast into the lake of fire. (14-15)

The dead, who were not found belonging to the *"book of life"* and the spirit of the age, were *"cast into the lake of fire"* where they suffer from spiritual depravation begotten of the *"second death."*

Revelation Chapter 21

Law of God

We have before explained [11:1-2, p. 105] that what is most frequently meant by the Holy City, the Jerusalem of God, which is mentioned in the Holy Book, is the Law of God. It is compared sometimes to a bride, and sometimes to Jerusalem, and again to the new heaven and earth. So in chapter 21, verses 1, 2 and 3 of the Revelation of St. John, it is said:[119]

And I saw a new heaven and a new earth: for the first heaven and the first earth were passed away; and there was no more sea. And I John saw the holy city, new Jerusalem, coming down from God out of heaven, prepared as a bride adorned for her husband. And I heard a great voice out of heaven saying, Behold, the tabernacle of God is with men, and he will dwell with them, and they shall be his people, and God himself shall be with them, and be their God. (1-3)

Notice how clear and evident it is that the first heaven and earth signify the former Law. For it is said that the first heaven and earth have passed away and there is no more sea - that is to say, that the earth is the place of judgment, and on this earth of judgment there is no sea, meaning that the teachings and the Law of God will entirely spread over the earth, and all men will enter the Cause of God, and the earth will be completely inhabited by believers; therefore, there will be no more sea, for the dwelling place and abode of man is the dry land. In other words, at that epoch the field of that Law will become the pleasure ground of man. Such earth is solid; the feet do not slip upon it.

---

[119] 'Abdu'l-Bahá, *Some Answered Questions,* Bahá'í Publishing Trust, Wilmette, Illinois, pp. 67-68.

The Law of God is also described as the Holy City, the New Jerusalem. It is evident that the New Jerusalem which descends from heaven is not a city of stone, mortar, bricks, earth and wood. It is the Law of God which descends from heaven and is called new, for it is clear that the Jerusalem which is of stone and earth does not descend from heaven, and that it is not renewed; but that which is renewed is the Law of God.

The Law of God is also compared to an adorned bride who appears with most beautiful ornaments, as it has been said in chapter 21 of the Revelation of St. John: *"And I John saw the holy city, new Jerusalem, coming down from God out of heaven, prepared as a bride adorned for her husband."*

No More Death

And God shall wipe away all tears from their eyes; and there shall be no more death, neither sorrow, nor crying, neither shall there be any more pain: for the former things are passed away. (4)

New teachings and laws, the basis for renewed morality, become the touchstone for behavior. In ancient times, the Law of God or Holy of Holies was safeguarded in the inner room of the tabernacle of God. Now, "The Lord God Omnipotent hath been enthroned in His Kingdom,"[120] promulgation of the Law of God within the outer court becomes a universal condition, "and all men will enter the Cause of God." [121]

> He hath wiped away their tears, kindled their light, rejoiced their hearts and enraptured their souls. Death [spiritual] shall no more overtake them neither shall sorrow, weeping or tribulation afflict them.[122]

---

[120] 'Abdu'l-Bahá, *Selections from the Writings of 'Abdu'l-Bahá,* Bahá'í World Center, Haifa, Israel. p.12.
[121] 'Abdu'l-Bahá, *Some Answered Questions,* Bahá'í Publishing Trust, Wilmette, Illinois, p. 67.
[122] 'Abdu'l-Bahá, *Selections from the Writings of 'Abdu'l-Bahá,* Bahá'í World Center, Haifa, Israel, p.12.

All Things New

And he that sat upon the throne said, Behold, I make all things new. And he said unto me, Write: for these words are true and faithful. (5)

Bahá'u'lláh is sitting on the throne of Revelation and brings teaching for this age. He makes *"all things new"* so that a sanctified humanity can enthusiastically participate in the building of the Kingdom of God manifested as a global society. John was instructed to write because these words are true and faithful. Clearly, mankind must be reborn to the needs of this age.

> 'Except a man be born of water and of the Spirit, he cannot enter into the Kingdom of God. That which is born of the flesh is flesh; and that which is born of the Spirit is spirit.' [John 3:56] The purport of these words is that whosoever in every dispensation is born of the Spirit and is quickened by the breath of the Manifestation of Holiness, he verily is of those that have attained unto 'life' and 'resurrection' and have entered into the 'paradise' of the love of God.[123]

And he said unto me, It is done. I am Alpha and Omega, the beginning and the end. I will give unto him that is athirst of the fountain of the water of life freely. He that overcometh shall inherit all things; and I will be his God, and he shall be my son.(6-7)

Those who overcome, p. 54, shall inherit all things and be God's son. Past religions (churches) are promised this reward by the Father. Of this event, 'Abdu'l-Bahá says,

> He [Bahá'u'lláh] is Alpha and Omega. He is the One that will give unto him that is athirst of the fountain of the water of life and bestow upon the sick the remedy of true salvation. He whom such grace aideth is verily he that receiveth the most glorious

---

[123] Baha'u'llah, *Kitáb-i-Íqán,* , Baha'i Publishing Trust, Wilmette, Illinois pp. 118.

heritage from the Prophets of God and His holy ones. The Lord will be his God, and he His dearly beloved son.[124]

Those who overcome and drink the spiritual waters are rewarded with eternal life.

> The meaning of eternal life is the gift of the Holy Spirit, as the flower receives the gift of the season, the air, and the breezes of spring. Consider: this flower had life in the beginning like the life of the mineral; but by the coming of the season of spring, of the bounty of the clouds of the springtime, and of the heat of the glowing sun, it attained to another life of the utmost freshness, delicacy and fragrance. The first life of the flower, in comparison to the second life, is death.[125]

The Second Death

But the fearful, and unbelieving, and the abominable, and murderers, and whoremongers, and sorcerers, and idolaters, and all liars, shall have their part in the lake which burneth with fire and brimstone: which is the second death. (8)

This age suffers from unwarranted attachment to materialism; man is in need of detachment from those things that separate him from firm life in the covenant. To miss this revelation and spiritual renewal is to suffer the second death. The unrelenting are condemned to a *"lake which burneth with fire and brimstone..."* for the material world lacks many spiritual values.

> The world for the most part is sunk in materialism, and the blessings of the Holy Spirit are ignored. There is so little real spiritual feeling, and the progress of the world is for the most part merely material. Men are becoming like unto beasts that perish, for we know that they have no spiritual feeling they do not turn to God,

---

[124] 'Abdu'l-Bahá, *Selections from the Writings of 'Abdu'l-Bahá*, Bahá'í Publishing Trust, Wilmette, Illinois, p. 13.
[125] 'Abdu'l-Bahá, *Some Answered Questions*, Bahá'í Publishing Trust, Wilmette, Illinois p. 242.

they have no religion! These things belong to man alone, and if he is without them he is a prisoner of nature, and no whit better than an animal. How can man be content to lead only an animal existence when God has made him so high a creature?[126]

The Lamb's Wife

And there came unto me one of the seven angels which had the seven vials full of the seven last plagues, and talked with me, saying, Come hither, I will show thee the bride, the Lamb's wife. (9)

John is invited by one of the angels of the seven last plagues to see the bride. The Bridegroom, the Lamb, is the Word of God, verses 19:11-13, p. 183. The Bride is the Holy City, New Jerusalem, and Law of God, p. 193, which brings revival to the outer court of verse 11:2, p. 105, or to the form, practice, and administration of religion. The world is in need of the Bride or Law of God because the outer court of religious practice, with lack of good will among diverse peoples, encompasses the entire earth; it is only becoming unified as it appeals to the revitalized Word of God.

That Great City

And he carried me away in the spirit to a great and high mountain, and showed me that great city, the holy Jerusalem, descending out of heaven from God, Having the glory of God: and her light was like unto a stone most precious, even like a jasper stone, clear as crystal; And had a wall great and high, and had twelve gates, and at the gates twelve angels, and names written thereon, which are the names of the twelve tribes of the children of Israel: On the east three gates; on the north three gates; on the south three gates; and on the west three gates. And the wall of the city had twelve foundations, and in them the names of the twelve apostles of the Lamb. And he that talked with me had a golden reed to measure the city, and the gates thereof, and the wall thereof. (10-15)

While in the spirit, John is carried to the high mountain of religious renewal from where he sees that great city descending out of heaven from God. About that city, the following description is given:

---

[126] 'Abdu'l-Bahá, *Paris Talks,* Bahá'í Publishing Trust, 27, Rutland Gate, London S.W. 7 p. 122.

The meaning of the passage is that this heavenly Jerusalem hath twelve gates, through which the blessed enter into the City of God. These gates are souls who are as guiding stars, as portals of knowledge and grace; and within these gates there stand twelve angels. By 'angel' is meant the power of the confirmations of God—that the candle of God's confirming power shineth out from the lamp niche of those souls—meaning that every one of those beings will be granted the most vehement confirming support.

These twelve gates surround the entire world, that is they are a shelter for all creatures. And further, these twelve gates are the foundation of the City of God, the heavenly Jerusalem, and on each one of these foundations is written the name of one of the Apostles of Christ. That is to say, each one maketh manifest the perfections, the joyous message, and the excellency of that holy Being.

In brief, the Scripture saith: 'And he that talked with me had a rod made out of gold, that is, a measure, wherewith he measured the city and the gates thereof and the towers thereof.' The meaning is that certain personages guided the people with a staff grown out of the earth, and shepherded them with a rod, like unto the rod of Moses. Others trained and shepherded the people with a rod of iron, as in the dispensation of Muhammad. And in this present cycle, because it is the mightiest of Dispensations, that rod grown out of the vegetable kingdom and that rod of iron will be transformed into a rod of purest gold, taken from out the endless treasure houses in the Kingdom of the Lord. By this rod will the people be trained.

Note well the difference: at one time the Teachings of God were as a staff, and by this means the Holy Scriptures were spread abroad, the Law of God was promulgated and His Faith established. Then followed a time when the staff of the true Shepherd was as iron. And today, in this new and splendid age, the rod is even as pure gold. How wide is the difference here! Know, then, how much ground hath been gained by the Law of God and His Teachings in this dispensation, how they have reached such heights that they far transcend the dispensations gone before: truly this rod is purest gold, while those of other days were of iron and wood. [127]

And the city lieth foursquare, and the length is as large as the breadth: and he measured the city with the reed, twelve thousand furlongs. The length and the breadth and the height of it are equal. And he measured the wall thereof, an hundred and forty and four cubits, according to the measure of a man, that is, of the angel. (16-17)

"*The length and the breadth and the height of it [the City] are equal.*" The City is a cube as is the holiest shrine of Islam, which is the Kaaba or Cube. Representing completeness, the city measures one thousand furlongs for each of the twelve tribes of Israel, for a total of twelve thousand furlongs, and joins them with Islam.

> His [Bahá'u'lláh] all conquering sovereignty is manifest; His all encompassing splendor is revealed. Beware lest thou hesitate or halt. Hasten forth and circumambulate the City of God that hath descended from heaven, the celestial Kaaba round which have circled in adoration the favored of God, the pure in heart, and the company of the most exalted angels.[128]

Acting with spiritual maturity, mankind is as an angel that becomes the measure of a man, his potential capacity.

---

[127] 'Abdu'l-Bahá, *Selection from the Writings of 'Abdu'l-Bahá,* Bahá'í World Center, Haifa, Israel. pp.166-167.
[128] Baha'u'llah, *Gleanings from the Writings of Bahá'u'lláh,* Baha'i Publishing Trust, Wilmette, Illinois. p. 16.

And the building of the wall of it was of jasper: and the city was pure gold, like unto clear glass. And the foundations of the wall of the city were garnished with all manner of precious stones. The first foundation was jasper; the second, sapphire; the third, a chalcedony; the fourth, an emerald; The fifth, sardonyx; the sixth, sardius; the seventh, chrysolyte; the eighth, beryl; the ninth, a topaz; the tenth, a chrysoprasus; the eleventh, a jacinth; the twelfth, an amethyst. And the twelve gates were twelve pearls: every several gate was of one pearl: and the street of the city was pure gold, as it were transparent glass. (18-21)

Further metaphoric terminology is presented on the qualities of the Holy City that generate the unity of mankind, a condition, which represents the culminating feature of social development. Spiritual qualities are figuratively represented by walls of jasper and gold, clear as glass; wall foundations employ all manner of precious stones, and each gate is as a pearl with streets of gold likened unto the clarity of glass.

'Haste thee, O Carmel!' Bahá'u'lláh, significantly addressing that holy mountain, has written, 'for lo, the light of the Countenance of God ... hath been lifted upon thee ... Rejoice, for God hath, in this Day, established upon thee His throne, hath made thee the dawning place of His signs and the dayspring of the evidences of His Revelation. Well is it with him that circleth around thee, that proclaimeth the revelation of thy glory, and recounteth that which the bounty of the Lord thy God hath showered upon thee.' 'Call out to Zion, O Carmel!' He, furthermore, has revealed in that same Tablet, 'and announce the joyful tidings: He that was hidden from mortal eyes is come!'[129]

The Glory of God

And I saw no temple therein: for the Lord God Almighty and the Lamb are the temple of it. And the city had no need of the sun, neither of the moon, to shine in it: for the glory of God did lighten it, and the Lamb is the light thereof. (22-23)

---

[129] Shoghi Effendi, *God Passes By*, Bahá'í Publishing Trust, Wilmette, Illinois, pp. 277-278,.

God, as represented by the Lamb, becomes the temple of the City; the Bahá'í Administrative System is responsible to, and reflects, the teachings of Bahá'u'lláh. Through this executive system, the laws and ordinances of God, contained in Bahá'u'lláh's Book of Laws known as the *Kitáb-I-Aqdas,*[130] shall be practiced, in the normal affairs of mankind, on a full-time basis.

The Word of God in the city is compared to the warmth and light of the sun and the reflection of the moon. Leaders of religion in the past have functioned as the sun and moon of spiritual teachings, but in this age the light of God is fully contained in the Word of God as reflected by Bahá'u'lláh, the Glory of God, the Lamb and Father. The Word is administratively protected.

It behoveth the loved ones of the Lord to be the signs and tokens of His universal mercy and the embodiments of His own excelling grace. Like the sun, let them cast their rays upon garden and rubbish heap alike, and even as clouds in spring, let them shed down their rain upon flower and thorn. Let them seek but love and faithfulness, let them not follow the ways of unkindness, let their talk be confined to the secrets of friendship and of peace. Such are the attributes of the righteous; such is the distinguishing mark of those who serve His Threshold.

The Abha Beauty endured the most afflictive of calamities. He bore countless agonies and ills. He enjoyed not a moment's peace, drew not an easeful breath. He wandered, homeless, over desert sands and mountain slopes; He was shut in a fortress, and a prison cell. But to Him, His pauper's mat of straw was an eternal throne of glory, and His heavy chains a sovereign's carcanet. By day, by night, He lived under a whirring sword, and He was ready from moment to moment for death on the cross. He bore all this that He might purify the world, and deck it out with the tender

---

[130] Bahá'u'lláh, *Kitáb-i-Íqán,* Bahá'í Publishing Trust, Wilmette, Illinois

mercies of the Lord God; that He might set it at rest; that conflict and aggression might be put to flight, the lance and the keen blade be exchanged for loving fellowship, malevolence and war turn into safety and gentleness and love, that battlefields of hate and wrath should become gardens of delight, and places where once the blood drenched armies clashed, be fragrant pleasure grounds; that warfare should be seen as shame, and the resort to arms, even as a loathsome sickness, be shunned by every people; that universal peace raise its pavilions on the loftiest mounts, and war be made to perish forever from the earth.[131]

Honor of the Nations

And the nations of them which are saved shall walk in the light of it: and the kings of the earth do bring their glory and honour into it. And the gates of it shall not be shut at all by day: for there shall be no night there. And they shall bring the glory and honour of the nations into it. (24-26)

Nations of them that are saved shall accept the teachings and walk in its light. Political leaders shall give praise to the city, and bring in the glory and honor of the nations that will never be without enlightenment.

The Revelation of Bahá'u'lláh, whose supreme mission is none other but the achievement of this organic and spiritual unity of the whole body of nations, should, if we be faithful to its implications, be regarded as signalizing through its advent the coming of age of the entire human race. It should be viewed not merely as yet another spiritual revival in the ever changing fortunes of mankind, not only as a further stage in a chain of progressive Revelations, nor even as the culmination of one of a series of recurrent prophetic cycles, but rather as marking the last and highest stage in the stupendous evolution of man's collective life on this planet. The emergence of a world community, the con-

---

[131] 'Abdu'l-Bahá, *Selection from the Writings of 'Abdu'l-Bahá,* Bahá'í World Center, Haifa, Israel. p. 257-258.

sciousness of world citizenship, the founding of a world civiliza-tion and culture all of which must synchronize with the initial stages in the unfoldment of the Golden Age of the Bahá'í Era should, by their very nature, be regarded, as far as this planetary life is concerned, as the furthermost limits in the organization of human society, though man, as an individual, will, nay must in-deed as a result of such a consummation, continue indefinitely to progress and develop.[132]

The Lamb's Book of Life

And there shall in no wise enter into it any thing that defileth, neither whatsoever worketh abomination, or maketh a lie: but they which are written in the Lamb's book of life. (27)

Its administrative structure shall prevent anything that *"defileth … worketh abomination, or maketh a lie"* to enter into it. Those who overcome are dressed in the white raiment of the law and ordinances for this age, and shall have their name in the Lamb's book of life, 3:5.

Material brotherhood does not prevent nor remove warfare; it does not dispel differences among mankind. But spiritual alliance destroys the very foundation of war, effaces differences entirely, promulgates the oneness of humanity, revivifies mankind, causes hearts to turn to the Kingdom of God and baptizes souls with the Holy Spirit. Through this divine brotherhood the material world will become resplendent with the lights of Divinity, the mirror of materiality will acquire its lights from heaven, and jus-tice will be established in the world so that no trace of darkness, hatred and enmity shall be visible. Humanity shall come within the bounds of security, the Prophethood of all the Messengers of God shall be established, Zion shall leap and dance, Jerusalem shall rejoice, the Mosaic flame shall ignite, the Messianic light

---

[132] Shoghi Effendi, *The World Order of Bahá'u'lláh*, Bahá'í Publishing Trust, Wilmette, Illinois p 163.

shall shine, the world will become another world, and humanity shall put on another power. This is the greatest divine bestowal; this is the effulgence of the Kingdom of God; this is the day of illumination; this is the merciful century. We must appreciate these things and strive in order that the utmost desire of the Prophets may now be realized and all the glad tidings be fulfilled. Trust in the favor of God. Look not at your own capacities, for the divine bestowal can transform a drop into an ocean; it can make a tiny seed a lofty tree. Verily, divine bestowals are like the sea, and we are the fishes of that sea. The fishes must not look at themselves; they must behold the ocean, which is vast and wonderful. Provision for the sustenance of all is in this ocean; therefore, the divine bounties encompass all, and love eternal shines upon all.[133]

---

[133] 'Abdu'l-Bahá, *Promulgation of Universal Peace,* Bahá'í Publishing Trust, Wilmette, Illinois, p.126-127.

Revelation Chapter 22

Tree of Life

And he showed me a pure river of water of life, clear as crystal, proceeding out of the throne of God and of the Lamb. In the midst of the street of it, and on either side of the river, was there the tree of life, which bare twelve manner of fruits, and yielded her fruit every month: and the leaves of the tree were for the healing of the nations. (1-2)

John was shown Spirit, the pure water of life that comes from the throne of the Prophet, Bahá'u'lláh, Who is the Lamb of this age.

> The testament of Bahá'u'lláh is a Rain of Goodness, a Sun of Truth, Water of Life, the Holy Spirit.[134]

> The tree of life is the highest degree of the world of existence: the position of the Word of God, and the supreme Manifestation.[135]

The power of the covenant is reflected in religious teachings that are renewed with each religious dispensation. The covenant preserves the water of life and nurtures the earth of men's hearts. Its hallmark in this age is for the development of spiritual maturity.

The tree of life was forbidden to mankind in the creation story. However, God provided for man's continued development. "[God] placed at the east of the Garden of Eden cherubim, and a flaming sword which turned every way, to keep the way of the tree of life." (Gen 3:24) Is not this "flaming sword" the Word of God sent forth as the sharp two-edged sword, v. 1:16, from the mouth of the Prophet, and "sent forth into all the earth..." by the Lamb?

Attributes of wisdom and spiritual maturity are required by all peoples in order to establish world peace. Otherwise, how can swords be beaten into

---

[134] 'Abdu'l-Bahá, *Paris Talks*, Bahá'í Publishing Trust, Wilmette, Illinois. p.172,
[135] 'Abdu'l-Bahá, *Some Answered Questions*, Bahá'í Publishing Trust, Wilmette, Illinois. p.124.

plowshares? Many fruits and leaves exist within the Bahá'í teachings. Some fruits for the healing of the nations are: the oneness of God, of mankind, and of religions; equality of sexes; an administrative system with consultative bodies; essential harmony of science and religion; an auxiliary universal language, world monetary system, international police force, and a federation of world states.

Leaves support and contribute to the growth and development of trees and their fruits. By analogy, it is probable that leaves refer to the administrative system, which is essential to the well being of the community. The Bahá'í Administrative System is inseparable from its teachings.

Only by study of the writings can one obtain a true feeling for the magnitude of social change and for the level of spiritual life to be attained because of the Revelation of Bahá'u'lláh.

> Who can doubt that such a consummation—the coming of age of the human race—must signalize, in its turn, the inauguration of a world civilization such as no mortal eye hath ever beheld or human mind conceived? Who is it that can imagine the lofty standard which such a civilization, as it unfolds itself, is destined to attain? Who can measure the heights to which human intelligence, liberated from its shackles, will soar? Who can visualize the realms which the human spirit, vitalized by the outpouring light of Bahá'u'lláh, shining in the plenitude of its glory, will discover?[136]

God and the Lamb

And there shall be no more curse: but the throne of God and of the Lamb shall be in it; and his servants shall serve him: And they shall see his face; and his name shall be in their foreheads. And there shall be no night there; and they need no candle, neither light of the sun; for the Lord God giveth them light: and they shall reign for ever and ever. (3-5)

All inhabitants of the city shall relate to the Law of God for this age. Their demeanor is a reflection of people that live in the spirit and radiance

---

[136] Shoghi Effendi, *The World Order of Bahá'u'lláh,* Bahá'í Publishing Trust, Wilmette, Illinois p 206.

of the Word of God for the light of the teachings gives them spiritual understanding.

> 'Followers of the Gospel,' Bahá'u'lláh addressing the whole of Christendom exclaims, 'behold the gates of heaven are flung open. He that had ascended unto it is now come. Give ear to His voice calling aloud over land and sea, announcing to all mankind the advent of this Revelation a Revelation through the agency of which the Tongue of Grandeur is now proclaiming: 'Lo, the sacred Pledge hath been fulfilled, for He, the Promised One, is come!' The voice of the Son of Man is calling aloud from the sacred vale: 'Here am I, here am I, O God my God!' ... whilst from the Burning Bush breaketh forth the cry: 'Lo, the Desire of the world is made manifest in His transcendent glory!' The Father hath come. That which ye were promised in the Kingdom of God is fulfilled. This is the Word which the Son veiled when He said to those around Him that at that time they could not bear it... Verily the Spirit of Truth is come to guide you unto all truth... He is the One Who glorified the Son and exalted His Cause... The Comforter Whose advent all the scriptures have promised is now come that He may reveal unto you all knowledge and wisdom. Seek Him over the entire surface of the earth, haply ye may find Him.[137]

Practice of teachings such as the oneness of religions and removal of prejudice will remove the curse of past social and economic injustices. All believers shall serve God and the Lamb by means of spiritual maturity gleaned from the light of universal teachings. *'[H]is name [spiritual quality] shall be in their foreheads,'* and there is no need for pastoral guidance. *"[F]or the Lord God giveth them light [voluminous teachings]: and they shall reign for ever and ever.'* Additional promises are presented in Chapters 2 and 3, p. 51.

Lord God of the Holy Prophets

And he said unto me, These sayings are faithful and true: and the Lord God of the holy prophets sent his angel to show unto his servants the things which must shortly be done. (6)

"The Lord God of the holy prophet" sent His Messenger for this age. By analogy, He is often compared to the physical sun.

> These Suns of Truth are the universal Manifestations of God in the worlds of His attributes and names, even as the visible sun that assisteth, as decreed by God, the true One, the Adored, in the development of all earthly things, such as the trees, the fruits, and colours thereof, the minerals of the earth, and all that may be witnessed in the world of creation, so do the divine Luminaries [Prophets], by their loving care and educative influence, cause the trees of divine unity, the fruits of His oneness, the leaves of detachment, the blossoms of knowledge and certitude, and the myrtles of wisdom and utterance, to exist and be made manifest... through the rise of these Luminaries of God the world is made new, the waters of everlasting life stream forth, the billows of loving kindness surge, the clouds of grace are gathered, and the breeze of bounty bloweth upon all created things... through the abundant grace of these Symbols of Detachment...the Spirit of life everlasting is breathed into the bodies of the dead.[138]

Behold, I come quickly: blessed is he that keepeth the sayings of the prophecy of this book. (7)

After two millennia the verse *"Behold, I come quickly..."* acquires a new significance. It becomes a literal truth from the time one finds Bahá'u'lláh as, for example, when he understands the significance of the Book of Revelation. The statement is a declaration from the speaker of the throne. Blessed are they who support His work.

Bahá'u'lláh says that a heavy burden, of responsibility, for *"keeping the sayings of the prophecy of this book"* lies with Kings and Rulers of the earth.

> We pray God -- exalted be His glory -- and cherish the hope that He may graciously assist the manifestations of affluence and power and the dayprings of sovereignty and glory, the kings of

---

[138] Bahá'u'lláh, *Kitáb-i-Íqán,* Bahá'í Publishing Trust, Wilmette, Illinois, p. 33-34.

the earth may God aid them through His strengthening grace to establish the Lesser Peace.[139]

[It will insure tranquility of the nations provided that sovereigns hold fast to the agreements. To achieve this end:] it is their duty to convene an all-inclusive assembly...[for the purpose of consultation.] They must put away the weapons of war, and turn to the instruments of universal reconstruction. Should one king rise up against another, all the other kings must arise to deter him.[140]

We beseech God to aid them to do His will and pleasure. He, verily, is the Lord of the throne on high and of earth below, and the Lord of this world and of the world to come...Any king who will arise and carry out this task, he, verily will, in the sight of God, become the cynosure of all kings. Happy is he, and great is his blessedness.[141]

Worship God

And I John saw these things, and heard them. And when I had heard and seen, I fell down to worship before the feet of the angel which showed me these things. Then saith he unto me, See thou do it not: for I am thy fellowservant, and of thy brethren the prophets, and of them which keep the sayings of this book: worship God. (8-9)

To worship Him, John fell at the feet of the angel who brought the message. *'See thou do it not...'* for *'I am thy fellow servant...worship God.'*

And since there can be no tie of direct intercourse to bind the one true God with His creation, and no resemblance whatever can exist between the transient and the Eternal, the contingent and the Absolute, He hath ordained that in every age and dispen-

---

[139] Bahá'u'lláh, *Epistle to the Son of the Wolf*, Bahá'í Publishing Trust, Wilmette, Illinois, p. 30.
[140] Ibid, pp. 30-31.
[141] Ibid, p. 31.

sation a pure and stainless Soul be made manifest in the king-doms of earth and heaven.[142]

Each Prophet brings the Word of God and is the way unto God for His dispensation. "Jesus saith unto him, I am the way, the truth, and the life: no man cometh unto the Father, but by me." (John 14:6)[143]

Keep This Book Open

And he saith unto me, Seal not the sayings of the prophecy of this book: for the time is at hand. He that is unjust, let him be unjust still: and he which is filthy, let him be filthy still: and he that is righteous, let him be righteous still: and he that is holy, let him be holy still. (10-11)

Do not conceal the meaning of this book for the time is at hand fol-lowed by the paraphrase—let men act on the basis of their own character and volition—provides an interesting plea for religious tolerance.

The heaven of true understanding, Bahá'u'lláh says, shineth re-splendent with the light of two luminaries: tolerance and right-eousness.[144]

O my friend! Vast oceans lie enshrined within this brief saying. Blessed are they who appreciate its value, drink deep therefrom and grasp its meaning, and woe betide the heedless. This lowly one entreateth the people of the world to observe fairness, that their tender, their delicate and precious hearing which hath been created to hearken unto the words of wisdom may be freed from impediments and from such allusions, idle fancies or vain imagin-ings as 'cannot fatten nor appease the hunger,' so that the true Counsellor may be graciously inclined to set forth that which is

---

[142] Bahá'u'lláh, *Bahá'u'lláh, Gleanings from the Writings of Bahá'u'lláh,* Bahá'í Publishing Trust, Wilmette, Illinois, p. 66.
[143] See Verses Rev 1:17, 19:4, 5 and 10.
[144] Bahá'u'lláh, *Tablets of Bahá'u'lláh,* Bahá'í Publishing Trust, Wilmette, Illinois, p. 169-170.

the source of blessing for mankind and of the highest good for all nations.[145]

Give Every Man

And, behold, I come quickly; and my reward is with me, to give every man according as his work shall be. (12)

Bahá'u'lláh reaffirms the statement of verse *7, "I come quickly..."* He adds that men will be rewarded *"according as his work shall be."*

> O My servant, who hast sought the good pleasure of God and clung to His love on the Day when all except a few who were endued with insight have broken away from Him! May God, through His grace, recompense thee with a generous, an incorruptible and everlasting reward, inasmuch as thou hast sought Him on the Day when eyes were blinded.[146]

"By faith is meant, first, conscious knowledge, and second, the practice of good deeds."[147] In this Dispensation, works are for the betterment of mankind.

God's Eternal Authority

I am Alpha and Omega, the beginning and the end, the first and the last. Blessed are they that do his commandments, that they may have right to the tree of life, and may enter in through the gates into the city. (13-14)

The Speaker declares his identity as the Father, and acknowledges the blessedness of those who do God's commandments.

> God has not created men that they should destroy one another. All races, tribes, sects and classes share equally in the Bounty of their Heavenly Father.

---

[145] Ibid, p. 170.

[146] Bahá'u'lláh, *Gleanings from the Writings of Bahá'u'lláh,* Bahá'í Publishing Trust, Wilmette, Illinois, p. 36.

[147] Bahá'u'lláh and 'Abdu'l-Bahá, *The Bahá'í World Faith,* Bahá'í Publishing Trust, Wilmette, Illinois p. 383.

The only difference lies in the degree of faithfulness, of obedience to the laws of God. There are some who are as lighted torches, there are others who shine as stars in the sky of humanity. The lovers of mankind, these are the superior men, of whatever nation, creed, or colour they may be. For it is they to whom God will say these blessed words, 'Well done, My good and faithful servants.' In that day He will not ask, 'Are you English, French, or perhaps Persian? Do you come from the East, or from the West?'[148]

Jesus Testifies

For without are dogs, and sorcerers, and whoremongers, and murderers, and idolaters, and whosoever loveth and maketh a lie. I Jesus have sent mine angel to testify unto you these things in the churches. I am the root and the offspring of David, and the bright and morning star. (15-16)

The Author of Revelation comments on the sordid affairs of the environment on the day of resurrection. On this same subject, Bahá'u'lláh has said:

> Grieve thou not over those that have busied themselves with the things of this world, and have forgotten the remembrance of God, the Most Great. By Him Who is the Eternal Truth! The day is approaching when the wrathful anger of the Almighty will have taken hold of them. He, verily, is the Omnipotent, the All Subduing, the Most Powerful. He shall cleanse the earth from the defilement of their corruption, and shall give it for an heritage unto such of His servants as are nigh unto Him.[149]

Jesus gave his revelation to John who was the angel who testified to the churches. The message of Revelation was sent and signified by an angel of God, the speaker on the throne. The Lamb precedes and follows (root and offspring) David, and is the bright and morning star of each new age. In

---

[148]'Abdu'l-Bahá, *Paris Talks,* Bahá'í Publishing Trust, 27, Rutland Gate, London S.W. 7, p.148-149.
[149] Bahá'u'lláh, *Gleanings from the Writings of Bahá'u'lláh,* Bahá'í Publishing Trust, Wilmette, Illinois, p. 208.

each Dispensation, the Lamb, as Prophet, is the dawning light of new revelation.

Water of Life

And the Spirit and the bride say, Come. And let him that heareth say, Come. And let him that is athirst come. And whosoever will, let him take the water of life freely. (17)

The bridegroom, the bride and those who hear, all invite others who thirst for the waters of life to join in and partake of the teachings for this age.

> Divine nearness is dependent upon attainment to the knowledge of God, upon severance from all else save God. It is contingent upon self sacrifice and to be found only through forfeiting wealth and worldly possessions. It is made possible through the baptism of water and fire revealed in the Gospels. Water symbolizes the water of life, which is knowledge, and fire is the fire of the love of God; therefore, man must be baptized with the water of life, the Holy Spirit and the fire of the love of the Kingdom. Until he attains these three degrees, nearness to God is not possible.[150]

Do not Add or Take Away

For I testify unto every man that heareth the words of the prophecy of this book, If any man shall add unto these things, God shall add unto him the plagues that are written in this book: And if any man shall take away from the words of the book of this prophecy, God shall take away his part out of the book of life, and out of the holy city, and from the things which are written in this book. He which testifieth these things saith, Surely I come quickly. Amen. Even so, come, Lord Jesus. (18-20)

The Father, *"Surely I come quickly,"* gives a warning: one should not add to or take away from the meaning of the Book of Revelation. Adding to or taking away from *"the words of the book of this prophecy,"* would be a mater of corrupting the text.

---

[150] 'Abdu'l-Bahá, *Promulgation of Universal Peace,* Bahá'í Publishing Trust, Wilmette, Illinois, p. 142.

Bahá'u'lláh explains that adding to or subtracting from the verses is not practical because of wide dispersion of the holy books. Corrupting the text is an outcome of improper interpretation:

This commentary is constructed upon the basis of information contained in the Bahá'í writings with limitations of accuracy as noted in the introduction, p. 23. The Book of Revelation uses much symbolism and metaphor and for this reason the following comment on the problem of interpretation from 'Abdu'l-Bahá is particularly meaningful to both the author and reader:

> Be not satisfied with words, but seek to understand the spiritual meanings hidden in the heart of the words. The Jews read the Old Testament night and day, memorizing its words and texts yet without comprehending a single meaning or inner significance, for had they understood the real meanings of the Old Testament, they would have become believers in Christ, inasmuch as the Old Testament was revealed to prepare His coming. As the Jewish doctors and rabbis did not believe in Christ, it is evident that they were ignorant of the real significance of the Old Testament. It is difficult to comprehend even the words of a philosopher; how much more difficult it is to understand the Words of God. The divine Words are not to be taken according to their outer sense. They are symbolical and contain realities of spiritual meaning. For instance, in the book of Solomon's songs you will read about the bride and bridegroom. It is evident that the physical bride and bridegroom are not intended. Obviously, these are symbols conveying a hidden and inner significance. In the same way the Revelations of St. John are not to be taken literally, but spiritually. These are the mysteries of God. It is not the reading of the words that profits you; it is the understanding of their meanings. Therefore, pray God that you may be enabled to comprehend the mysteries of the divine Testaments.[151]

---

[151] 'Abdu'l-Bahá, *Promulgation of Universal Peace,* Bahá'í Publishing Trust, Wilmette, Illinois, p 454-455.

God's Grace

The grace of our Lord Jesus Christ be with you all. Amen. (21)

The Speaker desires the grace of Lord Jesus Christ for everyone; testimony for the Book of Revelation is from Jesus Christ.

> This is the Day in which God's most excellent favors have been poured out upon men, the Day in which His most mighty grace hath been infused into all created things. It is incumbent upon all the peoples of the world to reconcile their differences, and, with perfect unity and peace, abide beneath the shadow of the Tree of His care and loving kindness. It behoveth them to cleave to whatsoever will, in this Day, be conducive to the exaltation of their stations, and to the promotion of their best interests. Happy are those whom the all glorious Pen was moved to remember, and blessed are those men whose names, by virtue of Our inscrutable decree, We have preferred to conceal.

> Beseech ye the one true God to grant that all men may be graciously assisted to fulfil that which is acceptable in Our sight. Soon will the present day order be rolled up, and a new one spread out in its stead. Verily, thy Lord speaketh the truth, and is the Knower of things unseen.[152]

* * *

The prospect of the future sees a world commonwealth that will emerge from out of present universal difficulties. On the road of transition, the world's people will suffer "carnage, agony, and havoc of this great world convulsion" ... whose "consummation will ... be a gradual process..." Change accompanied by numerous difficulties will:

> lead at first to the establishment of that Lesser Peace which the nations of the earth ... will themselves establish. This momentous

---

[152] Bahá'u'lláh, *Gleanings from the Writings of Bahá'u'lláh,* Bahá'í Publishing Trust, Wilmette, Illinois pp. 6-7.

and historic step ... [resulting from] universal recognition of its oneness and wholeness, will bring in its wake the spiritualization of the masses, ... [and the] ultimate fusion of all races, creeds, classes, and nations which must signalize the emergence of His New World Order.

Then will a world civilization be born, flourish, and perpetuate itself, a civilization with a fullness of life such as the world has never seen nor can as yet conceive ... will the planet, galvanized through the universal belief of its dwellers in one God, and their allegiance to one common Revelation, mirror, within the limitations imposed upon it, the effulgent glories of the sovereignty of Bahá'u'lláh, shining in the plenitude of its splendor in the Abha Paradise, and be made the footstool of His Throne on high, and acclaimed as the earthly heaven, capable of fulfilling that ineffable destiny fixed for it, from time immemorial, by the love and wisdom of its Creator.

The present duty of spiritual helpers:

however confused the scene, however dismal the present outlook...[is] to labor serenely, confidently, and unremittingly to ... [lead] humanity out of the valley of misery and shame to the loftiest summits of power and glory.[153]

---

[153] Shoghi Effendi, *The Promised Day is Come,* Bahá'í Publishing Trust, Wilmette, Illinois, pp.128-9.

The Chaining of the Dragon

Conclusions

The Prophets and Messengers of God have been sent down for the sole purpose of guiding mankind to the straight Path of Truth. The purpose underlying Their revelation hath been to educate all men, that they may, at the hour of death, ascend, in the utmost purity and sanctity and with absolute detachment, to the throne of the Most High. The light which these souls radiate is responsible for the progress of the world and the advance-ment of its peoples. They are like unto leaven which leaveneth the world of being, and constitute the animating force through which the arts and wonders of the world are made manifest. Through them the clouds rain their bounty upon men, and the earth bringeth forth its fruits.

Gleanings, pp. 156-157

Conclusions

Verses from within the Book of Revelation predict the return of Jesus Christ and speak about the glory of the renewed Law of God coming down from heaven at the time of His appearance and of worldwide spiritual renewal. Bahá'u'lláh declared:

> The time foreordained unto the peoples and kindreds of the earth is now come. The promises of God, as recorded in the holy Scriptures, have all been fulfilled. Out of Zion hath gone forth the Law of God, and Jerusalem, and the hills and land thereof, are filled with the glory of His Revelation. Happy is the man that pondereth in his heart that which hath been revealed in the Books of God, the Help in Peril, the Self-Subsisting.[154]

Accordingly, renewal of civilization, initiated by bestowal of the Bábí and Bahá'í Faiths, began in 1844 AD as promised. It is to their message that we must look when attempting to lay out aspects of the future. Voluminous Bahá'í writings, supporting humanity's approach to spiritual maturity, provide information and guidance required to establish a peaceful world civilization. Peace in this day is not only possible, but is assured. Bahá'u'lláh reminds us that man is a spiritual being, that past progress within the confines of civilization is the result of previous spiritual accomplishments, and that future progress will depend on renewal of the human spirit and acceptance of new social principles with applicability to these times.

Contrasting the age of Bahá'u'lláh's revelation, a social period that was still living in the dark ages of material convenience and technical achievements, to the present notable achievements provides insight as to the timeliness of revelation. This observation is particularly true in the fields of communication and travel where speed for either activity was but a few miles per hour. Modern communications make possible the real time dis-

---

[154] Bahá'u'lláh, *Gleanings from the Writings of Bahá'u'lláh,* Bahá'í Publishing Trust, Wilmette, Illinois, p.12-13.

semination of information, and this capacity for immediacy is important to and useful for dialogue at a global level. The social conditions of one and half centuries ago can also be contrasted with the world environment of the present Information Age. In the mid 19th-Century, the Industrial Age was still in its infancy. Colonialism, the offspring of world commerce, was the great enterprise of the age, the concept of empire was near its end, and Kingdoms and Dynasties were falling. Struggle for national power was becoming the great thrust of the times. The world still loomed large in the minds of men; resources seemed unlimited. National competition in the form of World Wars had not yet begun, but activities of the old order were leading toward the devastating military explosions of the 20th-Century. Great changes of the next 150 years, with the Spirit of a new age, would introduce innovations as confirmed by Bahá'u'lláh:

> Verily I say, whatever is sent down from the heaven of the Will of God is the means for the establishment of order in the world and the instrument for promoting unity and fellowship among its people.[155]

*　*　*

Thus it is seen that this age has new demands and responsibilities not only because of enlightenment coming from the spirit of new revelation but also because of the burgeoning power of the scientific method and connected advances of technology. Understanding of these new demands is essential to the central goal of forming a global society; particularly, in view of the inherent danger of recent material achievements. 'Abdu'l-Bahá has explained:

> Scientific knowledge is the highest attainment upon the human plane, for science is the discoverer of realities. It is of two kinds: material and spiritual. Material science is the investigation of natural phenomena; divine science is the discovery and realization of spiritual verities. The world of humanity must acquire both. A bird has two wings; it cannot fly with one. Material and spiritual science are the two wings of human uplift and attainment. Both

---

[155] Bahá'u'lláh, *Tablets of Bahá'u'lláh*, Bahá'í Publishing Trust, Wilmette, Illinois, p. 67.

are necessary - one the natural, the other supernatural; one material, the other divine. By the divine we mean the discovery of the mysteries of God, the comprehension of spiritual realities, the wisdom of God, inner significances of the heavenly religions and foundation of the law.[156]

Recent scientific achievements—though cause for additional responsibilities—have provided new information as regards the nature of the cosmos and have led to better understanding of totality. No longer is the universe seen as a mechanical system set in motion by its creator, definable in Cartesian coordinates, and left to wind down with the passing of time. Instead, the universe, becomes a living dynamic system of continuing evolution that gives birth and death to millions of stars. The cosmos, beyond understanding of man, demands a need for God, which we understand as being the Creative Force of the universe. Professing faith in this need, the universe can be studied as the Creator's work of art, and becomes a subject of unlimited beauty, variation, interest, and wonder, making for a powerful demonstration of the infinite capacity and purpose of its Motivating Force.

Humanity lives in a global habitat that is housed within its solar system near the edge of but one of millions of galaxies. Recent scientific understanding suggests a great need for the care of this habitat since it is a living organic system of which humanity is totally dependent for its life support. That care of the earth might be required was, in past times, an unthinkable idea. But with a tendency of overpopulation combined with the destructive powers of science, the necessity of a symbiotic relationship between mankind and the earth becomes apparent. Humanity, in respect to its everyday casual treatment of the earth, and as regards the extreme affect of some of its creations, is upsetting, or has upset the earth's living space which fact can be seen in the numerous forms of environmental disturbance.

Initiation of the space age, with its many spectacular accomplishments, has presented a new perspective about humanity's complete dependence on the well being of the space-based earth. Ever since 1969 when man went to the moon, all peoples have been able to see photographs of the earth from space. Astronauts even saw an *earth rise* from the moon. There is one obvious conclusion all can agree upon: our space ship, earth, rides the solar cir-

---

[156] 'Abdu'l-Bahá, *Promulgation of Universal Peace,* Bahá'í Publishing Trust, Wilmette, Illinois, p.133.

cuit steady as a rock, third planet from the sun, and has full dependence upon the latter body for its spatial position and life forms. The first dependency is in relation to the relative masses of the earth and the sun, and the second dependency is in respect to transmitted solar energy. Some reflection on how we inherited these dependencies is useful in contemplating responsibilities of the future.

For eons, the earth, initially as a non-living sphere, was bombarded with solar energy. Excitations from the sun's energy eventually led to molecules, subsequent life forms and the building of a biosphere surrounding the earth. This thin layer of marvelous complexity includes numerous species, their ecosystems, and operates through supportive combining relationships to provide for all life. Nature, at this level of development, is in perfect balance and self-sustaining. Living things within this world eat and are eaten, and this is a law of nature. But the system remains in tranquil balance only so long as it is undisturbed by different forces.

Humankind evolved from out of the earth's biosphere, but because of spiritual immaturity and freedom of will, has rebelled when it comes to care for the environment. Nevertheless, as science and space photography of the twentieth century have shown, life is dependent on maintaining the earth's living space, the biosphere: It provides the breath of life, and, though purchased in supermarkets, the food man eats. Maintenance of the biosphere is now one of his major responsibilities. But man, for lack of understanding and carelessness about it, is capable of markedly reducing the ability of the biosphere to maintain a viable habitat.

A tangible feel for human ability to compromise the biosphere can be visualized when one recognizes, with the use of some computations, there exists a per capita allowance of six acres of land for each individual of the world in consideration of our present population of about six billion people and a total land mass of approximately fifty seven million square miles.[157] The per capita portion of average allocation of land providing support to the biosphere must be reduced to a lesser figure because of existing cities, roads, commercial areas, pollution, waste fills, the destruction of vegetation, deserts, farming methods, etc. From this portrayal, one can see the tragic impasse coming from never ending population growth. By implication, humanity, with its ability to modify the natural balance of the earth's living

---

[157] Britannica

space, becomes, for preservation of survival, the de facto custodian for maintaining the health and balance of the earth's environment.

Two more material difficulties in need of spiritual solutions are apparent. Hunger for energy to feed the fires of modern industry and commerce are exhausting resources at a non-sustainable rate. For example, out of the biosphere there accumulated over a period of millions of years, reserves of stored energy such as coal, oil, and natural gas, but depletion of this available energy at its present rate of usage is foreseen within the first half of this century. The anticipated void represents a grave difficulty to the present pursuit of production and commercialism. In addition to its foreseeable insufficiency, its interim usage, contributing to the ashen content of the atmosphere, plays havoc with life sustaining qualities of the environment.

Scientific advancement opened the door to understanding of atomic energy and the nuclear bomb. Bahá'u'lláh had seen the difficulties of this discovery:

> Strange and astonishing things exist in the earth but they are hidden from the minds and the understanding of men. These things are capable of changing the whole atmosphere of the earth and their contamination would prove lethal. Great God![158]

This acquisition becomes another burdensome responsibility as both the bomb and the presence of nuclear matter, from both military and commercial use, have capability of destroying large portions of the biosphere. The latter possibility has already been demonstrated by the high cost to life and land from the event of the Russian accident at Chernobyl, and for thousands of years this generation has bequeathed an assignment burdened with care of spent nuclear fuel. By the grace of God a nuclear winter, initiated by out-of-control politics, has not thus far occurred.

* * *

The above material problems, along with many other social and economic inequalities, require spiritual solutions. A spiritual solution cannot be accomplished until mankind, by means of its own development, recognizes

---

[158] Bahá'u'lláh, *Tablets of Bahá'u'lláh,* Bahá'í Publishing Trust, Wilmette, Illinois, p. 69.

the deep-seated truth of the concept of the oneness of mankind. Shoghi Effendi explains that it is the sole means for salvation of the world:

> The proclamation of the Oneness of Mankind - the head corner-stone of Bahá'u'lláh's all-embracing dominion - can under no circumstances be compared with such expressions of pious hope as have been uttered in the past. ... It implies at once a warning and a promise - a warning that in it lies the sole means for the salvation of a greatly suffering world, a promise that its realization is at hand.[159]

Through appropriate training, man draws out the nature of his own true inner reality and becomes a spiritual being. This is mankind's point of commonality and the basis of the oneness of humanity, and this reality is owed to qualities and state of mind: *spirituality* is an accessible quality within reach of all people who discover God's Messenger, study His laws and ordinances, and attempt to practice them.

> [T]he mind is the power of the human spirit. Spirit is the lamp; mind is the light which shines from the lamp. Spirit is the tree, and the mind is the fruit. Mind is the perfection of the spirit and is its essential quality, as the sun's rays are the essential necessity of the sun.[160]

This capacity to assume spiritual qualities is open to all humanity and is in need of development until such time as the generality of thought accepts Bahá'u'lláh's pivotal teaching on the "oneness of mankind." Humanity is one, regardless of color, ethnic origin, or gender. A parallel thought is in need of emphasis because of the way women have been deprived throughout history of expressing their god-given qualities; namely, that the oneness of mankind implies the equality of men and women:

> In proclaiming the oneness of mankind He [Bahá'u'lláh] taught that men and women are equal in the sight of God and that there

---

[159] Bahá'u'lláh, *World Order of Bahá'u'lláh,* Bahá'í Publishing Trust, Wilmette, Illinois, p. 47.
[160] 'Abdu'l-Bahá, *Some Answered Questions*, Bahá'í Publishing Trust, Wilmette, Illinois p. 209.

is no distinction to be made between them. The only difference between them now is due to lack of education and training.[161]

Bahá'u'lláh viewed education, essential to the development of humanity, as a universal requirement applicable to all mankind. Learning about spiritual verities should derive largely from family example, participation in the Bahá'í Community, and from study of Bahá'í writings and other religious scriptures. Material education, including scientific study, should be of sufficient range to eliminate religious superstitions. Then the individual can make independent judgments without dependence on others. This capacity for discrimination is the basis of justice and leads to the unity of mankind:

The purpose of justice is the appearance of unity among men.[162]

By its aid [Justice] thou shalt see with thine own eyes and not through the eyes of others, and shalt know of thine own knowledge and not through the knowledge of thy neighbor. Ponder this in thy heart; how it behooveth thee to be.[163]

As 'Abdu'l-Bahá explained, the goal of Bahá'ís is to have the highest personal standards:

I desire distinction for you...You must become distinguished for loving humanity, for unity and accord, for love and justice. In brief, you must become distinguished in all the virtues of the human world - for faithfulness and sincerity, for justice and fidelity, for firmness and steadfastness, for philanthropic deeds and service to the human world, for love toward every human being, for unity and accord with all people, for removing prejudices and promoting international peace.[164]

[161] 'Abdu'l-Bahá, *Promulgation of Universal Peace,* Bahá'í Publishing Trust, Wilmette, Illinois, p. 169.
[162] Bahá'u'lláh, *Tablets of Bahá'u'lláh,* Bahá'í Publishing Trust, Wilmette, Illinois, p. 67
[163] Bahá'u'lláh, *The Hidden Words,* Bahá'í Publishing Trust, Wilmette, Illinois, p. 2.
[164] 'Abdu'l-Bahá, *Promulgation of Universal Peace,* Bahá'í Publishing Trust, Wilmette, Illinois, p. 185.

He made clear the need for work:

> In the Bahá'í Cause arts, sciences and all crafts are (counted as) worship . ... Briefly, all effort and exertion put forth by man from the fullness of his heart is worship, if it is prompted by the highest motives and the will to do service to humanity. This is worship: to serve mankind and to minister to the needs of the people. Service is prayer.[165]

Interaction between society and the individual, as with humanity and the environment, is cause for mutual dependencies. Shoghi Effendi explains:

> It is the duty of those who are in charge of the organization of society to give every individual the opportunity of acquiring the necessary talent in some kind of profession, and also the means of utilizing such a talent, both for its own sake and for the sake of earning the means of his livelihood. Every individual, no matter how handicapped and limited he may be, is under the obligation of engaging in some work or profession, for work, especially when performed in the spirit of service, is according to Bahá'u'lláh, a form of worship. It has not only a utilitarian purpose, but has a value in itself, because it draws us nearer to God, and enables to better grasp His purpose for us in this world. It is obvious, therefore, that the inheritance of wealth cannot make anyone immune from daily work.[166]

Thus it is seen, education, both spiritual and material, participation in community, and work become the means for the spiritual development of the individual, and as presented above constitute the ultimate purpose of the human endeavor. But need of support toward appropriate development resulted in the lack of drawing out full human potential and has led to frequent despair of the individual within the current social condition. Present attitudes, whatever their specific cause—such as "political ideology, academic elitism ... consumer economy, the 'pursuit of happiness,'"[167] all fos-

---

[165] 'Abdu'l-Bahá, *Paris Talks*, Bahá'í Publishing Trust, Wilmette, Illinois. p.176.
[166] Shoghi Effendi, *Directives of the Guardian*, Bahá'í Publishing Trust, New Delhi, p. 83.
[167] Bahá'í internal document, *"Who is Writing the Future."*

ter social disunity, and have led to devastating conditions of society where the social illness is seen from symptoms of drugs, guns, school shootings, gangs, and scandals in and out of institutions. And this situation seems a universal condition.

Correction to these difficulties demands that society and governments recognize the reality of humanity—that people are spiritual beings, but in need of social and economic support so that they can bring out the full potential of their true nature and thereby contribute to the well being of community. Support in the development of people requires recognition of individual needs in the various phases of life's development and cessation. As suggested, this places an obligation on society and the structure of government to make available to all persons appropriate education, and provisions for work. Not only this, misfortunes of life and the inevitability of old age require special considerations for the continued security of people and their society.

Slow development in the direction of life's continuation and care for the individual as a responsibility of the social structure can be seen from the early effort of religious experience and later by the workings of the social system. Christian tithes, charitable donations, and the Islamic zakat have been used for care of the unfortunate from early times. From the early 16th-Century, German towns and communities gave support to the needy by means of poor laws. By the end of that century, Elizabethan Poor Laws provided social assistance within England. Another means of social support, though limited to its own members, was provided by a system of guild collection boxes. These early endeavors for social support were not without fault, and it was not until the 19th-Century that, drawing on past experience, early forms of social insurance, as in Germany, were introduced. Significantly, need to cover medical, funeral, care of the disabled, illness, and health and accident expenses, were developing. Similar progress toward support of the individual was developing in various other European and South American countries.

Social programs were given a boost because of the great depression, which followed the economic crash after WWI. Experimentation of that period included the concepts of "the just wage" and family allowance; greater participation of European and South American countries occurred, and this period initiated various programs within the United States. Present day Social Security originated in 1935, government provided employment through the Work Progress Administration, and numerous other programs supported needs of various kinds.

Weakening of the nuclear family as the building block of society paralleled transfer from an agrarian to an industrial society. Disruption of the family in these times can be seen by the attitudes of individuals who have new freedoms without balance of agreed upon social responsibilities and by economic systems requiring employment of both husband and wife. The trend toward irresponsible individualism seems maximized at the present.

A similar injurious characteristic applicable to modern day nation-states exists. National sovereignty, the expression of individualism among nation-states, has led to warfare and ideological conflicts of the past century and seems an anachronous and administratively deficient condition in these times of instant world-wide communication, an international economy, and need for global organization.

* * *

Erecting a society that provides a viable way of life involves the obvious need for correction of present difficulties, but perhaps foremost, change requires an admission of the general prevailing sickness as assessed by Bahá'u'lláh:

> Regard the world as the human body which, though at its creation whole and perfect, hath been afflicted, through various causes, with grave disorders and maladies.[168]

Today, all major problems are global because spiritual and material difficulties of similar nature exist in most all countries; generally, their solution requires corrections internal to homeland and cooperation among the nations of the world. For various reasons, this situation has been evolving within humanity's evolutionary struggle toward greater organization. The need for this age is that of global agreements under the flag of unity. Toward this end, Bahá'ís see, as an initial condition, a world commonwealth growing out of political necessity. Transition toward that state requires continuing changes in human affairs.

---

[168] Bahá'u'lláh, *Gleanings from the Writings of Bahá'u'lláh,* Bahá'í Publishing Trust, Wilmette, Illinois, p. 254-255.

Significantly, humanity is building toward a global civilization. At the present time, if nothing else is cause for this direction of progress, the forces of international commerce when combined with the fear of modern engines of destruction, are forcing the issue. Bahá'u'lláh refers to this method of promotional interests as the "Lesser Peace."

> We pray God - exalted be His glory - and cherish the hope that He may graciously assist the manifestations of affluence and power and the dayprings of sovereignty and glory, the kings of the earth - may God aid them through His strengthening grace - to establish the Lesser Peace. This, indeed, is the greatest means for insuring the tranquility of the nations. It is incumbent upon the Sovereigns of the world - may God assist them - unitedly to hold fast unto this Peace, which is the chief instrument for the protection of all mankind.[169]

A preliminary Alliance of Nations as demonstrated by the United Nations will continue to progress into the future as a champion of human rights and into functioning as an international police force until such time as political peace is established. This tentative formation will in future centuries reach a flourishing condition in which its environment deserves the title of "Most Great Peace." Bahá'u'lláh explained to a visiting British Orientalist, Prof. Edward G. Browne:

> That all nations should become one in faith and all men as brothers; that the bonds of affection and unity between the sons of men should be strengthened; that diversity of religion should cease, and differences of race be annulled - what harm is there in this? ... Yet so it shall be; these fruitless strifes, these ruinous wars shall pass away, and the "Most Great Peace" shall come.... Do not you in Europe need this also? Is not this that which Christ foretold?[170]

* * *

---

[169] Bahá'u'lláh, *Epistle to the Son of the Wolf,* Bahá'í Publishing Trust, Wilmette, Illinois, p. 30
[170] (Peace, p. 157)

Many signs as regards the unification of all mankind do exist because of modern day activities all pointing to greater bonds of oneness. Scientific and material gains, providing enhanced means for communications, gradually appeared concurrently with the release and progress of God's word in the Bahá'í revelation. Bahá'í writings often refer to the past century as the "Century of Light" because of its phenomenal release of energy and motivating power toward both spiritual and material advancements. From within both regions humanity has been given tools for creating a global society: Spiritual information is contained in the Bahá'í writings, and material achievements are available from the tremendous progress of science.

Scientific progress in the form of the computer and the Internet make most knowledge available to anyone who can connect to this system. This factor serves as a great equalizer conducive to greater unity. It empowers the oppressed and weakens the power of self-serving factions that often times have covert leanings in promotion of their own ends. Perhaps that is why Non Governmental Organizations are becoming so important to bodies such as the United Nations. The NGOs are able to transcend political boundaries in their presentation of global issues. In any event, as seen from some research of the internet on global issues, International Governmental Agencies often times recommend closer ties and greater input from NGOs.

In recognition of the need for resolution of many global issues—sustainable development, biodiversity, chemical management, climate and atmosphere, desertification, forests, need for universal democracy, habitat, health issues, intergovernmental organizations, oceans and coasts, population, social development, trade and environment, wetlands, wildlife, rights of women—are all being discussed on the bases of Regional or International Forums, Conferences, and Summits. Some of these are being negotiated at an accelerating rate.

The recent trend toward interfaith cooperation provides an example of growing awareness about need for discussion of global issues. The first Parliament of the World Religions was held in Chicago, Illinois in 1893. This meeting marked the first announcement of the Bahá'í Revelation on the North American Continent. The second Parliament of the World Religions was held in Chicago in 1993, and the latest meeting occurred in Cape Town, South Africa in 1999. A document was prepared as a result of the second meeting in Chicago known as *Towards a Global Ethic: An Initial Declaration*. This document addressed four fundamental issues: non-violence and respect for life, solidarity and a just economic order, tolerance and a life of truthfulness, and equal rights and partnership between men an women.

The document was incorporated within *A Call to Our Guiding Institutions,* which was distributed at the Cape Town Conference of 1999. "A Call to Our Guiding Institutions is not a prescriptive or admonitory document. It is instead an appeal for active, ongoing dialogue about the creation of a just, peaceful, and sustainable future on behalf of the entire Earth community."[171]

Some progress develops only as a result of much suffering. This can be seen in the evolution of worldwide institutions. One of the first moves in the direction of world peace occurred in 1899 by the Tsar of Russia who was concerned about international instability within Europe. This and another conference in 1907 were held at The Hague, The Netherlands. Forty-four countries sent delegates to the second conference. One of the goals was to use arbitration to settle international disputes. Many proposed arrangements for regulating international disputes included: the rights of neutral nations, treatment of undefended towns, use of poison gases, and air warfare. Unfortunately, not all participating countries ratified the agreements. Another goal was to limit armaments, but Germany refused to partake of this discipline, and this among other reasons, resulted in World Wars II and I.

In spite of the apparent failure, any observer of these early efforts for peace can see the direction that was being advocated by participating world leaders. For example, another outgrowth of these early attempts was establishment of the Permanent Court of Arbitration known as The Hague Court.

Most people know World War I started in the contentious regions of the Balkans because of mixed religious and political loyalties. This calamitous struggle was followed by formation of the League of Nations—interestingly, an advocate of its creation was President Woodrow Wilson—but the rogue nation refusing to ratify its formation and give full support was none other than the United States. The World Court established by the League of Nations was superseded by The Hague Court. The idea of world peace was a continuing effort. But sometimes the affairs of men move slowly.

---

[171] *A Call to Our Guiding Institutions*

Without the support of the United States, the League of Nations failed to accomplish its immediate goals, but history has a way of moving mankind toward its preordained destiny. Following the great suffering of World War II, an environment of hope and need developed so that once more an engine of peace was established in the form of the United Nations. Though imperfect, it represents another step toward world unity. Supplementing its formation and as a result of the unfriendliness of Russia following World War II, NATO was formed. Now it is central to policing Europe and some of the Middle East. Since the fall of the Berlin Wall in 1989, even the Russians, support the effort of NATO at times. The direction of progress seems apparent.

Collective security, as with NATO, protects the participating countries from entering into combat with one another; mutual contribution to NATO is currently maintaining the peace of Europe. Although the United States provided the lion's share of military force in the Gulf War against Saddam Husayn and Iraq, the power of a mutually supported policing force was amply demonstrated by this six-day war. The concept can be extended to an international policing force and used to maintain peace among the nations of the world. For example:

> [P]eace demandeth that the Great Powers should resolve, for the sake of the tranquillity of the peoples of the earth, to be fully reconciled among themselves. Should any king take up arms against another, all should unitedly arise and prevent him. If this be done, the nations of the world will no longer require any armaments, except for the purpose of preserving the security of their realms and of maintaining internal order within their territories. This will ensure the peace and composure of every people, government and nation. We fain would hope that the kings and rulers of the earth, the mirrors of the gracious and almighty name of God, may attain unto this station, and shield mankind from the onslaught of tyranny.[172]

In respect to this concept of mutual security, the Universal House of Justice has explained:

---

[172] Bahá'u'lláh, *Gleanings from the Writings of Bahá'u'lláh,* Bahá'í Publishing Trust, Wilmette, Illinois, p. 249.

On the societal level, the principle of collective security enunciated by Bahá'u'lláh ... and elaborated by Shoghi Effendi ... does not presuppose the abolition of the use of force, but prescribes 'a system in which Force is made the servant of Justice,' and which provides for the existence of an international peace-keeping force that 'will safeguard the organic unity of the whole commonwealth.' ... Bahá'u'lláh expresses the hope that 'weapons of war throughout the world may be converted into instruments of reconstruction and that strife and conflict may be removed from the midst of men.'[173]

To resolve these many issues of international relations, Bahá'u'lláh, while under banishment from Persia, advocated the holding of a universal conference. Leaders of governments or their representatives "must needs attend it, and, participating in its deliberations, must consider such ways and means as will lay the foundations of the world's Great Peace amongst men."[174]

Progressive activities toward fulfillment of this bidding have been advancing, with increasing occurrences since WWII, because of NGO conferences and various UN activities. Beginning in 1998, the Secretary-General, Kofi Annan, advocated the holding of a UN Summit in the year 2000. This meeting he proposed should be preceded by a Millennium Forum comprising diverse NGOs from around the world and which have as their major purpose the gathering of ideas and recommendations in respect to the future of the United Nations in the 21st-Century. For the following two-year period numerous regional and international forums were held until, in May, 2000, the Millennium Forum was held at the United Nations. Approximately 1350 participants, from over 100 countries, represented more than 1000 NGOs. A final declaration, articulating "the views of civil society on six main themes of the Millennium Forum: peace, security and disarmament; eradication of poverty; human rights; sustainable development and the environment; globalization; and the strengthening and democratizing of the UN,"[175] was submitted to the Millennium Summit in September, 2000.

---

[173] Bahá'u'lláh, Kitáb-i-Aqdas, Bahá'í Publishing Trust, Wilmette, Illinois, Note 173, pp. 239-240.
[174] Bahá'u'lláh, *Proclamation of Bahá'u'lláh,* Bahá'í World Center, Haifa, Israel, pp. 115.
[175] Daily Journal, May 2000.

* * *

Assuredly, the new spirit and new understanding, as testified by Jesus Christ in the Book of Revelation, will at the appropriate time be manifested as World Peace in a Global Society. The following two paragraphs, bringing both hope and concern about those features of social environment generally associated with the promised Millennium, are taken from a publication by the Universal House of Justice entitled *The Promise of World Peace:*

> The Great Peace towards which people of good will throughout the centuries have inclined their hearts, of which seers and poets for countless generations have expressed their vision, and for which from age to age the sacred scriptures of mankind have constantly held the promise, is now at long last within the reach of the nations. For the first time in history it is possible for everyone to view the entire planet, with all its myriad diversified peoples, in one perspective. World peace is not only possible but inevitable. It is the next stage in the evolution of this planet--in the words of one great thinker, 'the planetization of mankind'.

> Whether peace is to be reached only after unimaginable horrors precipitated by humanity's stubborn clinging to old patterns of behavior, or is to be embraced now by an act of consultative will, is the choice before all who inhabit the earth. At this critical juncture when the intractable problems confronting nations have been fused into one common concern for the whole world, failure to stem the tide of conflict and disorder would be unconscionably irresponsible.

Appendix

Fulfilled Prophesies

Prophecy about God's Cause that speaks of a time of fulfillment began as far back as 2500 years ago. Anticipation of the future gave mankind hope because predictions looked for better things to come. Exactly what the promised future entails has never been understood with ample agreement. One key to further enlightenment on this subject comes from prophecy as presented in the Books of Daniel, Leviticus, and Revelation.

The general predictive procedure seems as follows: Historical event x is separated from historical event y by a prophesied time span. If significant events x and y can be found that agree with a predicted time span and also match a plausible interpretation, the conjecture adds support to that particular understanding. This conclusion is especially convincing when numerous prophecies from different eras and sources—Daniel, Leviticus, and Revelation—all agree with an interpretive model; for example, when events and time spans said to fulfill prophecies from Daniel are in agreement with events and spans from the Books of Leviticus and Revelation. Agreement of this sort, not only adds credibility to the interpretation, but also, if accepted as true understanding, demonstrates the power of the Spirit behind prophecy coming from God's Prophet.

This commentary, while explaining the Book of Revelation, attempts to show that the same discussion serves to explain prophecies of Daniel and Leviticus, all of which pertain to the advancement of God's Cause for the past two millennia. The key to this understanding was provided by 'Abdu'l-Bahá's "Table Talks," which are presented in *Some Answered Questions*.

Rules of interpretation for time-span use days, weeks, months, and years as measures of time. The terms are interchangeable. A *year* can be substituted for a *day* and then becomes *three hundred and sixty days* or *years*. A *week* can signify *seven days or seven years*. The concept is based on Numbers 14:34 which reads "After the number of the days in which ye searched the land, even forty days, each day for a year, shall ye bear your iniquities, even forty years, and ye shall know my breach of promise." The usual standards[176] are: a *week* equals *seven days;* a *month* equals *thirty days;* a *year* equals *three hundred sixty days.* Therefore a day can equal a year, which equals three hundred sixty days, which equals three hundred sixty years, etc. Another measure is *time* and *times* used respectively as one and two years, or as converted to days the periods yield values of 360 or 720 days, or again, as many years. The proper use of these measures must ultimately depend on the context.

'Abdu'l-Bahá has shown a pattern of time-span relationships that give meaning to prophecies from the Book of Revelation. He also explains the meaning of symbolic terms of the Book of Revelation and shows their consistency with the same time spans. Much of his explanation of both timing and symbolism centers on the history and internal conditions of the Faith of Islam; his explication also points to the birth of the Bahá'í Era. The Bar Chart, Figure 1, p. 243, demonstrates a consistent pattern of prophecies that support the historic position of the Faith of Islam and its contribution to the births of the Bábí and Bahá'í Faiths; coordinate with Table 1, p. 242.

- Note that the numbered *squares* at the ends of the bar diagrams, Figure 1, refer to the *row numbers* in Table 1 and thereby identify historic events with respect to prophesied time spans.

- For example, *Square 5* on the left end of the *fourth bar* from the top represents 677 BC, the Captivity of Manasseh, and relates to a nominal time span of 2520 years as discussed below.

- *Square 4* at the right end of the same bar represents 1844 AD, and marks the end of the Islamic Dispensation, the declaration of the Báb, and the beginning of spiritual renewal.

- The span, 5 to 4, is a period of *seven times* which equals seven years or 7x360, equals *2520 days* or *years,* and is interpreted to mean *2520 years.* This period is forecast in Leviticus, 26:18 and 24.

- The sum of 677 and 1844 equals 2521 years. The error of one year is attributable to precise date relations, and/or the difficulties of transition from reckoning time from BC to AD.

Why was this date relating to Manasseh chosen? Some review of Hebrew history offers clarification. The idea of Kingdom in Hebrew development started with Saul and David. The Kingdom continued with Solomon but began to deteriorate during his reign. After his death, the Kingdom di-

---

[176] Halley's Bible Handbook and others, and as used by 'Abdu'l-Bahá, *Some Answered Questions,* Bahá'í Publishing Trust, Wilmette, Illinois 60091, Chapter 10.

vided into Israel and Judah. Manasseh was the second king of Judah after the fall of Samaria and end of Israel.

The political and spiritual state of the Hebrews was from the time of Manasseh in a state of turmoil. Following centuries saw the dominant period of the Major and Minor Prophets and the time period when the Hebrews became identified as Jews. Detailed explanation for selection of the capture of Manasseh as the appropriate reference is provided in *I Shall Come Again.*[177] His captivity is used as the critical point in the decline of the Hebrew Nation, and this is consistent with the nature of the prophecy.

- The span 3 to 4 (upper right corner) accounts for the *391 year* period between the fall of Constantinople and the Báb's declaration at the end of the Islamic Dispensation, and refers to Revelation 9:15. The earlier date, 1453 AD, marks the end of the Roman Empire, which was the champion of Eastern Orthodox Christianity, and the latter date, 1844 AD, marks the end of the Islamic Dispensation as noted above.

- *Square 1*, the *first bar,* represents the third edict to rebuild Jerusalem, and *square 2* represents 33 AD, the Crucifixion of Jesus Christ, Daniel 9:24. From the time of the edict to rebuild Jerusalem to the Martyrdom of Christ there was a span of *seventy weeks* of years. Seven times seventy equals four hundred and ninety days or years. There were four edicts by three kings: Cyrus in the year 536 BC, first chapter of Ezra; Darius in the year 519 BC, sixth chapter of Ezra; Artaxerxes in the year 457 BC, seventh chapter of Ezra; Artaxerxes in the year 444 BC, second chapter of Nehemiah. Daniel refers to the third edict in 457 BC. Christ suffered martyrdom in 33 AD. Adding 457 and 33 years gives 490 years which agrees with Daniel's prophecy of seventy weeks, or 7 times 70 equals 490 days or years.

- The *second bar* confirms this interpretation, Daniel 9:25, 26. Daniel mentions *seven weeks* and *sixty-two weeks.* Seven weeks, or forty-nine days or years were used for the rebuilding of Jerusalem. Sixty-two weeks from the completion of Jerusalem the Messiah was "cut off". Seven weeks plus sixty-two weeks make sixty-nine weeks and His martyrdom was in the seventieth week, which agrees with the previous seventy weeks. These prophecies establish the third edict of 457 BC as a base line that agrees with the circumstance of the martyrdom of Christ.

- The *third bar* connects the Christian reference, 457 BC, *square 1,* with the Islamic and Bahá'í reference of 1844 AD, *square 4,* Daniel 8:13, 17,

---

[177]Hushidar Motlagh, *I Shall Come Again,* Global Perspective, Mt. Pleasant, Michigan, p. 328.

"how long shall be the vision concerning the daily sacrifice, and the transgression of desolation..." (13) *"... unto* **two thousand and three hundred days***; then shall the sanctuary be cleansed..." (14) "...Understand, O son of man: for at the* **time of the end** *[emphasis added] shall be the vision."* (17) Twenty three hundred days or 2300 years, from the base year of 457 BC brings the prediction to the year of 1844. At the time of the end, in the year 1844 the sanctuary will be cleansed. This prophecy is referring to the "last days" of the Muslim *generation* when it gives birth to the Bábí Revelation—then will the sanctuary be cleansed. Cleansing of the sanctuary is one of the primary functions of new revelation.

- *Square 6.* From Daniel 12:6, 7; *"How long shall it be to the end of these wonders?"* (6) *"the man clothed in linen...sware by him that liveth for ever that it shall be for* **a time, times, and an half***; and when he shall have accomplished to scatter the power of the holy people, all these things shall be finished."* (7) A time (year) plus times (two years) plus an half (half year) make three and a half times or three and a half years which equals *1260 days or 1260 years.* From the Hegira, which marks the beginning of the Muslim lunar calendar, to the declaration of the Báb are 1260 lunar years.

- In the Book of Revelation, this time span is referenced by seven different verses. All references become 1260 years by the same conversion procedures and refer to verses from Chapters 11, 12, and 13 of the Book of Revelation as noted on the Bar Chart. These time spans represent the *lunar* years from the Hegira to the declaration of the Báb in 1260 AH, which is 1844 AD.

- *Squares 7 and 8* connect the declaration of Muhammad with the declaration of Bahá'u'lláh, Daniel 12:11. *"And from the time that the daily sacrifice shall be taken away, and the abomination that maketh desolate set up, there shall be* **a thousand two hundred and ninety days***."* By the same procedure this prophecy refers to 1290 lunar years; the time from the declaration of Muhammad (to His wife Khadíjah and Ibn Nawfal ten years before the Hegira) to the declaration of Bahá'u'lláh in 1280 AH. The latter date is the year 1863 AD.

- *Squares 9 and 10* connect two institutions of peace being the Truce of al Hudaybíyyah with the formation of the Universal House of Justice, *"Blessed is he that waiteth, and cometh to* **the thousand three hundred and five and thirty days***,"* Daniel 12:12. This span becomes *thirteen hundred thirty five years.* The Universal House of Justice was formed in 1963 AD; it is the International Administrative and Supreme Executive and Spiritual Body of the Bahá'í Faith and resides on Mount Carmel in Haifa, Israel. The time span measures from Muhammad's agreement for Pilgrimage to Mecca in 628 AD, known as the Truce of al-Hudaybíyyah.

Figure 1, as discussed above, demonstrates the historic position of Islam and its association with the births of the Bábí and Bahá'í Faiths as prophesied. This connection affirms the continuity of God's Cause and places emphasis on a condition not fully understood in past religious studies. The difficulty arises, at least in part, from the situation explained in the following:

One of the historic problems of the World's Great Religions has been the lack of detail instruction about official administrative guidance and authority following the death of the Prophet-Founder. Consequently, all the Great World Religions, sooner or later, have become segmented. In this age, when world unity is the goal, the Báb and Bahá'u'lláh and Their appointed successors have set forth a clear delineation of authority. For more than its first century, the Faith enjoyed protection forthcoming from continued revelation and guidance from its carefully appointed Leaders.

Further details about the Bahá'í Era, Figure 2, p. 245, demonstrate the continuing authority of its Covenant and Administration throughout the periods of its Heroic and Formative Ages. The Figure provides visual details about periods of ministry and administration leading to the election of the Universal House of Justice. The apparent gap in Figure 2 from the martyrdom of the Báb in 1850 to the declaration of Bahá'u'lláh, in 1863, as prophesied successor by the Báb's own hand, is explained below, as is the gap from the death of Shoghi Effendi in 1957 to the first election of the Universal House of Justice in 1963. The following brief historical review helps to explain the resolute process of guidance existing within the Bahá'í Faith until such time as this administrative body was formed.

The ministry of the Báb, precursor to Bahá'u'lláh, lasted but six years and was terminated because of Persian religious and secular leaders. Initial response to the Báb's message was such that twenty thousand early believers were martyred because of their loyalty to this newborn faith. During the critical years, from the martyrdom of the Báb in 1850 until Bahá'u'lláh declared His mission in 1863, the Bábí Community of believing followers were in a state of disarray because of the loss of their Prophet-Founder and were therefore forced to carry on in a weakened state. About two years following the martyrdom of the Báb, His followers were caught up in a wave of persecution, p. 18. An indirect result of this reign of terror was the incarceration of Bahá'u'lláh in the Síyáh-Chál, a dungeon also known as the Black Pit of Tehran. It was under these conditions that He received the first foreshadowing of His role as God's promised Prophet or Manifestation for this Age. Following release from the dungeon He was banished from His native country of Persia to Baghdad where He remained for ten years. Both before Bahá'u'lláh's incarceration in the Síyáh-Chál, as in the Conference of Badasht, and during the years of His banishment to Baghdad, where He made His formal declaration in 1863, Bahá'u'lláh was able to indirectly guide the remnants of the Báb's followers. Guidance while in Baghdad resulted largely because of the influence Bahá'u'lláh had on visiting Bábís from Persia. Strengthening of the Bábí community in this way became the source of rejuvenated strength of the Bábí Faith until the time of His outward declaration and departure from Baghdad in 1863 AD, or the year 19 BE of the Bahá'í Era.

For the remainder of His banishment, Bahá'u'lláh's eldest son, 'Abdu'l-Bahá, now nineteen years of age, was a constant aide and support to Him. Generally enjoying more freedom than His Father, 'Abdu'l-Bahá was often times the only contact with the outside world and was held in highest esteem by His Father who referred to him as the 'Most Great Branch,' 'Mystery of God,' or the 'Master.' He enjoyed a special station, and by will and testament of Bahá'u'lláh was made the center of the Covenant. This Station, unique in the annals of religion, provided continuity to the Faith at the time of the death and spiritual ascension of Bahá'u'lláh in 1892.

'Abdu'l-Bahá was the perfect embodiment of his Father's Teachings, a perfect Bahá'í in action and blessed with complete understanding of Bahá'í Teachings. He it was, Who by His commentary, which declares the presence of the Islamic, Bábí and Bahá'í Faiths as partial content of the of the Book of Revelation,[178] opened the door to its general understanding. In the year 1912, he spent 239 days proclaiming Bahá'u'lláh's Teaching from New York to California. He was knighted at a special ceremony held in Haifa at the residence of the British Governor. This was done in recognition for his relief of suffering in the Holy Land during WW I. It was a title that he never used. His ministry lasted until the time of his death and spiritual ascension in 1921.

Shoghí Effendi, grandson of 'Abdu'l-Bahá, was made Guardian of the Faith by the will and testament of his grandfather. He was not only expected to guide the Faith and be its authorized interpreter, but was bur-

---

[178] 'Abdu'l-Bahá, *Some Answered Questions,* Bahá'í Publishing Trust, Chapters 10-13.

dened with the difficulty of dealing with covenant breakers, those who worked against the Faith of which some arose from the ranks of Bahá'u'lláh's own family. The magnitude of his inherited duties and the burden of troublemakers made the transition to new leadership a critical period. 'Abdu'l-Bahá's younger sister by three years, Bahíyyih Khánum, known as the Greatest Holy Leaf, rallied the believers around Shoghi Effendi during this difficult period and transfer of authority. Shoghi Effendi, but 25 years of age, was overwhelmed by his inherited responsibilities; he therefore took a year's leave to Switzerland where he could reflect and pray about his duties and approach to the future. He committed the affairs of the Faith, during this interval, to the guidance and protection of Bahíyyih Khánum.

Shoghí Effendi's ministry lasted from 1921 until his death in 1957. It was a period in which administration of the Faith was forming under his guidance and the Faith was expanding throughout the continents and regions of the earth.

An institution known as the Hands of the Cause was begun by Bahá'u'lláh and carried on by 'Abdu'l-Bahá and Shoghi Effendi. Serving individuals were selected for their high level of spiritual development and concern and care for the well being of the Faith. Following the death of Shoghi Effendi in 1957, these individuals preserved the unity of the Faith until such time as an elected group of their members could arrange for the first election of the Universal House of Justice in 1963. By this time there had developed a sufficient Bahá'í World Community, administratively organized Bahá'í believers throughout the world, to justify the election. The Universal House of Justice holds permanent residence at the Bahá'í World Center on the slopes of Mount Carmel.

Bahá'í elections are conducted without electioneering. In October of each year every Bahá'í District elects one or more delegates that in April elect a National Assembly for each nation, territory or island. Every five years, all members of National Assemblies gather in one place to elect the Universal House of Justice. Elected Bahá'ís at any organizational level are obliged to serve in office.

Table 1

1)	457 BC	Command to build Jerusalem
2)	33 AD	Crucifixion of Jesus Christ
3)	1453 AD	Fall of Constantinople
4)	1844 AD	Declaration of the Báb
5)	677 BC	Captivity of Manasseh
6)	622 AD	Hegira (Beginning of Muslim Calendar)
7)	612 AD	Declaration of Muhammad
8)	1863 AD	Declaration of Bahá'u'lláh
9)	628 AD	Truce of al-Hudaybiyyah
10)	1963 AD	Formation of Universal House of Justice

Spans 6-4 and 7-8 are in lunar years.
Note: Row numbers correspond with numbered "squares" of Figure 1

Figure 1-Prophetic Time Spans

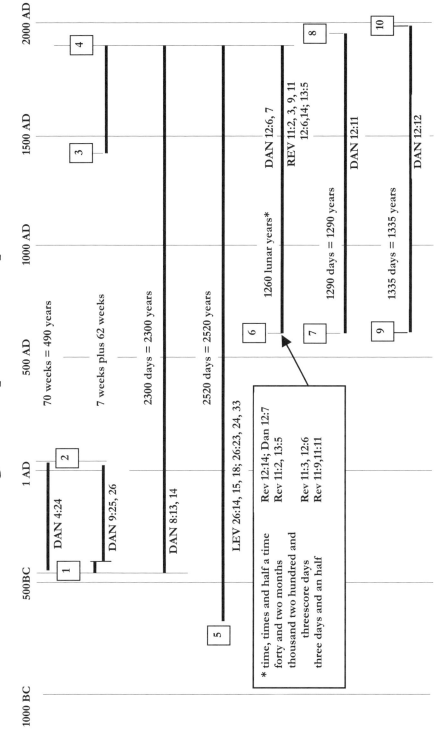

1000 BC · 500BC · 1 AD · 500 AD · 1000 AD · 1500 AD · 2000 AD

1 · **2** · **3** · **4** · **5** · **6** · **7** · **8** · **9** · **10**

DAN 4:24

DAN 9:25, 26

70 weeks = 490 years

7 weeks plus 62 weeks

DAN 8:13, 14 — 2300 days = 2300 years

2520 days = 2520 years

LEV 26:14, 15, 18; 26:23, 24, 33

1260 lunar years*

DAN 12:6, 7

REV 11:2, 3, 9, 11
12:6,14; 13:5

1290 days = 1290 years — DAN 12:11

1335 days = 1335 years — DAN 12:12

* time, times and half a time   Rev 12:14; Dan 12:7
  forty and two months   Rev 11:2, 13:5
  thousand two hundred and   Rev 11:3, 12:6
  threescore days
  three days and an half   Rev 11:9,11:11

243

It is of interest to note that Bahá'í development as an organized body, although guided by the writings of the Prophet, was, as regards material growth, a grass roots project. Under the guidance of the Báb, Bahá'u'lláh, 'Abdu'l-Bahá, and later of Shoghi Effendi, the Bahá'í revelation was taken throughout the world and administratively organized into a worldwide community. Those who joined the Faith were instrumental in building the electoral structure that elects the Universal House of Justice. Guidance to the World Community of Bahá'ís now derives from this Supreme Executive and Spiritual Body whose members are obliged to uphold, as principles of operation, the concepts held in the Bahá'í writings.

All Bahá'í Administrative Bodies function on the basis of consultation; forthcoming decisions represent a consensus view. Therefore authority is vested in the Body as a whole and not in one individual.

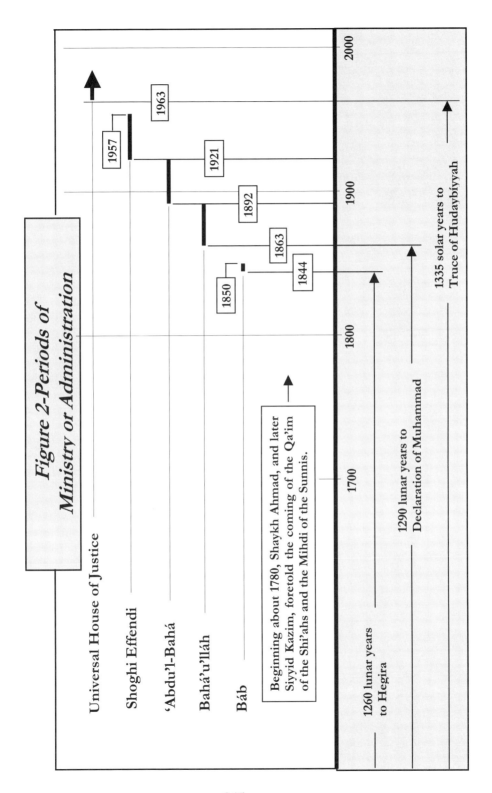

Figure 2-Periods of Ministry or Administration

Universal House of Justice

Shoghi Effendi

'Abdu'l-Bahá

Bahá'u'lláh

Báb

Beginning about 1780, Shaykh Ahmad, and later Siyyid Kazim, foretold the coming of the Qa'im of the Shi'ahs and the Mihdi of the Sunnis.

1260 lunar years to Hegira

1290 lunar years to Declaration of Muhammad

1335 solar years to Truce of Hudaybiyyah

1700
1800
1844
1850
1863
1892
1900
1921
1957
1963
2000

Index

twelve hundred and sixty years, 106
twenty-four, 117, 181
Twenty-four elders, 60, 61
two witnesses, 108
two-edged sword, 50, 205

U

Umayyads, 93, 111, 122, 129, 131, 136
Umayyah, 91
unified and peaceful world, 159
United Nations, 102, 162, 229, 232, 233
unity, 20, 46, 64, 82, 89, 102, 146, 159, 200
Universal House of Justice, 20, 232, 234, 238
universal Manifestation, 117, 208
universal peace, 66-68
Ushidar-Mah, 53

V

vain imaginings, 151
veils, 22, 44
vested powers, 64, 77, 142

W

warfare, 74, 159, 201, 228
warrior, 91, 94, 133
water, 110
waters, 50, 83, 141, 151, 156
white raiment, 57, 203
white stone, 56
winepress, 143, 144, 145
witness, 44, 157, 174
Witness, 108
woman, 121, 122, 165, 167, 177
word, 77

Word of God, 43, 50, 53, 55, 64, 81, 124, 125, 142, 172, 174, 184, 197, 200, 205
World Center, 20
world civilization, 202, 206
world commonwealth, 215, 228
world condition, 150, 171, 174
world peace, 48, 205, 231
World Peace, 234
world unity, 21, 48, 187, 232
worldly beasts, 75
wrath, 77, 108, 120, 143, 147, 149, 150, 159, 162, 201

Y

Yahyá, 154, 156, 157, 158, 159
Yazíd, 132, 133, 134, 135, 136

Z

Zachariah, 49
Zoroastrian, 28, 53